The Smithsonian Guides to Natural America

THE FAR WEST

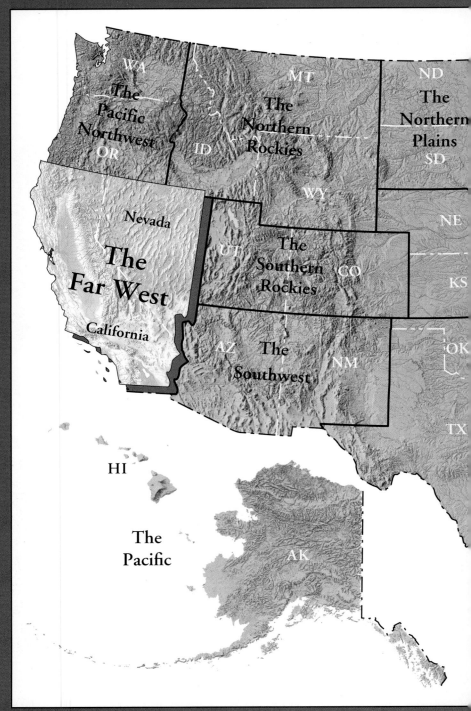

WA

The
Pacific
Northwest
OR

MT

The
Northern
Rockies

ID

ND

The
Northern
Plains
SD

Nevada

The
Far West

WY

UT

The
Southern
Rockies

CO

NE

KS

California

AZ

The
Southwest

NM

OK

TX

HI

The
Pacific

AK

MN

WI

MI

The
Great
Lakes

IA

The
Heartland

IL

IN

OH

MO

Central
Appalachia

KY

TN

The
South
Central
States

AR

MS

AL

The
Southeast

GA

LA

FL

Northern
New
England

ME

VT

NY

The
Mid-Atlantic
States

NH

MA
CT RI

Southern
New
England

NJ

PA

WV

MD

VA

The
Atlantic
Coast

NC

SC

THE FAR WEST
CALIFORNIA – NEVADA

THE SMITHSONIAN GUIDES TO NATURAL AMERICA

THE FAR WEST

CALIFORNIA AND NEVADA

TEXT

Dwight Holing

SPECIAL PHOTOGRAPHY

Len Jenshel and Diane Cook

PREFACE

Thomas E. Lovejoy

SMITHSONIAN BOOKS • WASHINGTON, D.C.
RANDOM HOUSE • NEW YORK, N.Y.

Front cover: East Anacapa Island, Channel Islands National Park, California
Half-title page: Sea otter opening clam on rock
Frontispiece: Foxtail pines, Kern Canyon, Sequoia National Park, California
Back cover: Prickly pear cactus fruit; Valley of Fire, Nevada; mountain lion

THE SMITHSONIAN INSTITUTION
SECRETARY I. Michael Heyman
COUNSELOR TO THE SECRETARY FOR BIODIVERSITY
AND ENVIRONMENTAL AFFAIRS Thomas E. Lovejoy
ACTING DIRECTOR, SMITHSONIAN INSTITUTION PRESS Daniel H. Goodwin
SMITHSONIAN BOOKS
EDITOR IN CHIEF Patricia Gallagher
SENIOR EDITOR Alexis Doster III
MARKETING MANAGER Susan E. Romatowski
BUSINESS MANAGER Steven J. Bergstrom
THE SMITHSONIAN GUIDES TO NATURAL AMERICA
SERIES EDITOR Sandra Wilmot
MANAGING EDITOR Ellen Scordato
PHOTO EDITOR Mary Jenkins
ART DIRECTOR Mervyn Clay
ASSISTANT PHOTO EDITOR Ferris Cook
ASSISTANT PHOTO EDITOR Rebecca Williams
ASSISTANT EDITOR Seth Ginsberg
COPY EDITORS Helen Dunn, Karen Hammonds
FACT CHECKER Jean Cotterell
PRODUCTION DIRECTOR Katherine Rosenbloom

Library of Congress Cataloging-in-Publication Data
Holing, Dwight.
    The Smithsonian guides to natural America. The Far West—
California and Nevada/ text by Dwight Holing; photographs by Len
Jenshel; preface by Thomas E. Lovejoy
      p. cm.
    Includes bibliographical references (p 262) and index.
    ISBN 0-679-76473-9 (pbk.)
    1. Natural history—California—Guidebooks 2. Natural history—
Nevada—Guidebooks 3. California—Guidebooks 4. Nevada—
Guidebooks. I. Title.
QH105.C2H64 1996   95-17457
508.794—dc20   CIP

Manufactured in the United States of America
98765432

HOW TO USE THIS BOOK

The SMITHSONIAN GUIDES TO NATURAL AMERICA explore and celebrate the preserved and protected natural areas of this country that are open for the public to use and enjoy. From world-famous national parks to tiny local preserves, the places featured in these guides offer a splendid panoply of this nation's natural wonders.

Divided by state and region, this book offers suggested itineraries for travelers, briefly describing the high points of each preserve, refuge, park or wilderness area along the way. Each site was chosen for a specific reason: Some are noted for their botanical, zoological, or geological significance, others simply for their exceptional scenic beauty.

Information pertaining to the area as a whole can be found in the introductory sections to the book and to each chapter. In addition, specialized maps at the beginning of each book and chapter highlight an area's geography and geological features as well as pinpoint the specific locales that the author describes.

For quick reference, places of interest are set in **boldface** type; those set in **boldface** followed by the symbol ❖ are listed in the Site Guide at the back of the book. (This feature begins on page 269, just before the index.) Here noteworthy sites are listed alphabetically by state, and each entry provides practical information that visitors need: telephone numbers, mailing addresses, and specific services available.

Addresses and telephone numbers of national, state, and local agencies and organizations are also listed. Also in appendices are a glossary of pertinent scientific terms and designations used to describe natural areas; the author's recommendations for further reading (both nonfiction and fiction); and a list of sources that can aid travelers planning a guided visit.

The words and images of these guides are meant to help both the active naturalist and the armchair traveler to appreciate more fully the environmental diversity and natural splendor of this country. To ensure a successful visit, always contact a site in advance to obtain detailed maps, updated information on hours and fees, and current weather conditions. Many areas maintain a fragile ecological balance. Remember that their continued vitality depends in part on responsible visitors who tread the land lightly.

C ONTENTS

PREFACE

The most fabulous part of natural America is its Far West: It ranges from the lowest point of North America (Death Valley, 282 feet below sea level) to the grand majesty of the Sierra, but its *ne plus ultra* is Yosemite. This valley was first entered by nonindigenous Americans at the beginning of the 1850s. Visitors to the area (including the painter Albert Bierstadt in 1863) told tales of its beauty so remarkable—and came in such numbers—that Abraham Lincoln took time in 1865, amid the Civil War, to cede Yosemite and its sequoias to the state of California for public use, resort, and recreation. But for the political peculiarities framing this farsighted act, Yosemite, and not Yellowstone, might have been the world's first national park.

This is the country of extraordinary naturalist John Muir. The resonance between its natural wonders and his genius has reverberated across the United States and beyond. His account *My First Summer in the Sierras* (1911) endures as one of the greatest nature books of all time. The Far West also encompasses the coastline of John Steinbeck, who wrote from Monterey, perched at the edge of its deep submarine canyon. The waters of this coastline are home to awesome kelp forests—where 300-foot-long brown algae seem to echo the towering coastal redwoods—as well as elephant seals, sea otters, and sea lions. Along this continental margin, gray whales seem to spout in salute as they make their way north and south. One can also greet an avian cornucopia of shorebirds, seabirds, and birds of prey (even peregrine falcons) as they gather at key staging areas on the Pacific Flyway. Off the coast, the sparkling waters of the Pacific are set with island jewels, such as the Farallons in the north or the Channel Islands in the south, where pygmy mammoths once held sway.

Far from devoid of life—"altogether valueless," as it was described by an early explorer—is the desert country that lies to the south and east of the Sierra in California and Nevada. To the contrary, the Sonoran, or low desert, features cool oases of California fan palms, the lipstick blossoms of ocotillo, and Anna's and Costa's hummingbirds.

PRECEDING PAGES: *In Nevada's stark Silver Peak Range, clouds as textured as the ground below skim over the volcanic badlands near Coaldale.*

The Mojave—so-called high desert despite the presence of Death Valley—offers to the observant visitor desert tortoises, desert pupfish that live in 111-degree Fahrenheit water fives times as salty as the sea, the Joshua tree, and other wildlife and plants. Nevada's Great Basin, profiled by John McPhee in his 1980 book *Basin and Range* and interspersed with wetlands such as Pyramid and Ruby lakes, hosts a constellation of wildflowers mirrored by the hues of birds such as lazuli buntings, violet-green swallows, and yellow-breasted chats.

Northern California and the eastern Sierra contain country shaped by fire and ice, as a visit to Mammoth Mountain or the quiescent volcano of Lassen Peak will instantly confirm. With Nevada, northern California shares Tahoe, the largest alpine lake in North America (and second largest in the world). A deep body of crystalline water, it was once seriously endangered by development but is now less so. I have enduring memories of a luminescent summer evening followed by a moonlit reverie on a smaller lake nearby. Here, too, is Mono Lake, shrunken victim of California water wars and the insatiable thirst of growing Los Angeles. Today the lake, with its dramatic tufa formations, is somewhat restored and more able to support its brine shrimps, a unique brine fly, and birds such as the snowy plover and the California gull.

Along the coast near Fort Bragg is a feature known as the Ecological Staircase, a series of terraces each older and higher than the previous. The Sierra Nevada (Snowy Range in Spanish) provides the real ecological staircase, however, rising from beach to snowbank, from chaparral through fir and pine, to alpine heathers and phlox within hours. This mighty range, which John Muir felt better deserved being called the "Range of Light" than of snow, is home not only to Yosemite but also to 66 glaciers and snowpacks, 16 major rivers, and more than 500 summits two miles high or more.

The consequence of all the Far West's geological and ecological variety is a biological profusion without parallel within the rest of the nation. From vernal pools to sand dunes, the Far West harbors numbers of species—particularly endemic species—beyond compare, including the oldest and largest living trees.

The story, however, is not one of a peaceable kingdom, because the Far West's natural areas have been reduced dramatically since the

---

OVERLEAF: *Albert Bierstadt painted this spectacular view of Yosemite Valley in 1868 following an 1863 overland journey into the Far West.*

era of the 49ers. Wilderness area has decreased by 80 percent and grass-lands by 99 percent. Nor is that all of the story: A horde of exotic species of plants and animals have taken hold to the disadvantage of native ones. The California condor, an awkward bird on the ground but one that I can attest is spectacularly graceful on the wing, clings to sur-vival only through herculean efforts. Some species, such as the Xerces blue butterfly, are gone forever. In fact, California is the only state to have an extinct animal, the California grizzly, on its flag; the last individ-ual died in captivity at San Simeon, the William Randolph Hearst estate.

California is also the site of one of the most important U.S. exper-iments in conservation. In the five southern counties, in an unprece-dented collaboration, federal agencies, state agencies, and counties, as well as development and environmental interests, are participating in natural community planning to preserve the coastal sage and its unique biota, including the California gnatcatcher. This is largely a voluntary exercise and its preliminary successes bode well for the ecosystem management approach to conservation.

For modern-day 49ers who recognize that biological wealth is the foundation for the future, the Far West is not only a natural mother lode with such wonders as the acorn woodpecker and the Coachella fringe-toed lizard, which literally swims through sand dunes. The re-gion may also be the place that shows us all how conservation and local aspirations can collaborate harmoniously. Even in the crowded mecca of Yosemite, one can find peace and beauty of wilderness: I once camped there for three days—but a mile from a main road—with nary an intruder to break natural America's glorious spell.

—Thomas E. Lovejoy
Counselor to the Secretary for
Biodiversity and Environmental Affairs,
SMITHSONIAN INSTITUTION

LEFT: *Annual winter rains transform the barren brown California desert with a burst of spring color. Here morning light illumines the sand dunes and evening primroses at Anza-Borrego Desert State Park.*

CALIFORNIA

PART ONE

C A L I F O R N I A

The nuggets of the 1849 gold rush are not the only wealth to earn California its nickname of the Golden State. Golden images are everywhere, from the cottonwood leaves that shade river canyons in autumn to the native bunchgrasses that carpet the vast valleys and in winter turn the foothills as tawny as mountain-lion coats, from the poppies that bloom in wild profusion each spring to the color that the beaches turn in a summer sunset.

Indeed, the Golden State is a veritable treasure chest of biological riches, brimming with coins of the natural realm. It exceeds every other region in the continental United States in species richness, ecological diversity, and rate of endemism, the occurrence of species found naturally nowhere else on earth. The oldest, the largest, and the tallest living things on earth grow in California, which also boasts the biggest wetland on the West Coast, the nation's largest mountain lake, the longest contiguous wall of granite in the world, the highest point in 49 states, and the lowest point in all 50.

Manifesting California's species richness are the estimated 7,850 kinds of vascular plants—one third of them endemic—that grow there, more than in the entire central and northeastern United States and adjacent Canadian provinces combined. Nonvascular flora push the floristic count even higher—1,000 to 1,200 lichens, 4,000 to 5,000 gilled fungi, 300 to 400 slime molds, and 600 to 700 mosses and liverworts. Of the 2,300 vertebrate species found in the country, 748 live in California. Endemism is rampant: 38 percent of the freshwater fish, 29 percent of the amphibians, and 9 percent of the mammals are native to this state and no place else. Their names

PRECEDING PAGES: *Striking vistas of sea-lashed rocky outcroppings framed by gnarled branches of wind-sculpted Monterey cypress make the Point Lobos State Reserve a favorite among painters and photographers.*

OREGON

Crescent
City

Siskiyou Mtns

Mt Shasta
14162

Coast Range

Red Bluff

Sacramento Valley

SIERRA

NEVADA

Lake
Tahoe

★ SACRAMENTO

PACIFIC

San Francisco

San Francisco Bay

San
Jose

Santa Cruz

Monterey Bay

Monterey

Santa Lucia Range

San Joaquin

NEVADA

Mono
Lake

CALIFORNIA

Valley

OCEAN

Bakersfield

CALIFORNIA
NORTH

50   0   50 Miles

50   0   50 Kilometers

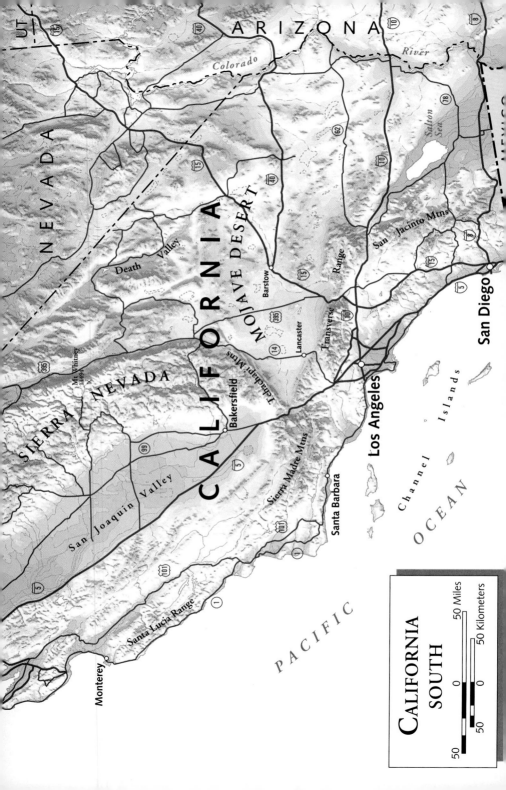

read like a California atlas: Kern River rainbow trout, Yosemite toad, San Diego Mountain king snake, San Joaquin kit fox, Buena Vista Lake shrew, Point Reyes mountain beaver, Los Angeles pocket mouse, Mojave ground squirrel. California also buzzes, hums, squirms, and crawls with nearly 30,000 different species of insects.

One reason for California's wealth of species is its dizzying selection of living quarters. Within the 11 biogeographic regions recognized by the state Department of Fish and Game, scientists have identified 396 distinct habitats, ranging from a rocky intertidal zone to an alpine fell field, from desert wash to old-growth redwood forest.

That so many types of habitat fall within California's boundaries is partially explained by the state's size and location. At 101,563,500 acres, California is the third-largest state in the union (only Alaska and Texas are bigger). It stretches 800 miles from Oregon in the north to Mexico in the south, and 200 miles across, from the Pacific Ocean to the deserts of Nevada and Arizona.

Within this sprawling landmass that rises from sea level to ski level in just two hours by car are rugged offshore islands, 1,100 miles of scalloped coastline, vast saltwater estuaries, a huge inland valley, 8 major mountain ranges containing more than 100 individually named mountain chains, 500 peaks that tower more than 2 miles high, 2 large dormant volcanoes and a host of cinder cones, 2 watersheds that are each larger than the state of New Hampshire, 5,000 lakes, 30,000 miles of rivers and streams, 40 million acres of forest land, and goodly chunks of 3 distinct deserts. Surely creating relief maps of the state is a cartographer's greatest challenge.

How such a variety of landforms came to be packed within 158,000 square miles is a story of unfathomable geologic force and power that is constantly unfolding, as attested by the devastating earthquake that wreaked havoc on Los Angeles in the early hours of January 17, 1994. Picture the earth's crust as a series of enormous jigsaw puzzle pieces. These plates, as scientists call them, are constantly moving. Two plates, the North American and Pacific, are slamming against each other off the continent's western edge like a pair of giant sumo wrestlers. The tectonic temblors they set off, which frequently rattle California, are only tiny indications of the force of this colossal collision. For hard evidence, turn to the state's coastal mountain ranges or the towering Sierra Nevada. Like folds and wrinkles in skin rubbed with a thumb, they are the result of the plates pushing against each other over millions of years.

California's landscape has been further defined by the rise and fall of sea levels, the coming and going of glaciers, and the cooling and warming of global temperature. Wind, rain, and erosion have left their mark as well. In naturalist and conservationist John Muir's beloved Yosemite Valley, for example, all the forces of nature have had a hand in creating one of the most beautiful artworks in the world.

Soil type, elevation, and amount of water are other factors in habitat type, as is weather. Along with only a handful of places worldwide and no others in North America, California has a Mediterranean climate. Besides mild, wet winters and warm, dry summers, a Mediterranean climate tends to nurture large numbers of endemic species. California is no exception.

Another element contributing to the Golden State's wealth of species is its relative isolation. In many ways California is an island, sequestered from the rest of the world by the Pacific Ocean on the west and a forbidding wall of granite bordered by desert on the east. Within this island are hundreds of smaller geographic islands isolated by environmental barriers such as rivers and mountains. Because California's isolating geographic features were created over millions of years by dynamic and acutely active geologic forces, resident flora and fauna underwent speciation by evolving new genetically regulated characteristics. Two species of tui chub, finger-length minnows found in two widely separated stream systems in eastern California, illustrate this process. Until 10,000 years ago they belonged to one continuous population. Sometime after the last Ice Age, a gradual warming of the re-

RIGHT: *Lush bracken and sword ferns, which thrive in the moist coastal climate, carpet the Lady Bird Johnson Grove in Redwood National Park.*
OVERLEAF: *Its shape may resemble a small cub, but the golden-spined Teddy Bear cholla at Joshua Tree National Park is not exactly cuddly.*

8

ABOVE: *Enduring symbol of the west coast, the California brown pelican has made a comeback after DDT exposure brought it close to extinction.*

gion dried up the waterways connecting the two streams. In the resulting isolation, the fish evolved into two genetically distinct subspecies.

Not all of California's biological excess is so positive, however. Along with the great numbers of flora and fauna species and habitat types, California is by far the most populous state, home to more than one out of ten Americans. It is also among the fastest growing, with a population that increased 26 percent between the early 1980s and early 1990s. Los Angeles, for example, grew by three million people during this period. The heavy toll on the environment can be measured by the loss of natural habitat and the increase in pollution.

Consider these statistics: California has lost 99 percent of its native grasslands, 94 percent of its inland wetlands and 80 percent of its coastal wetlands, 80 percent of its wilderness, and 89 percent of its riparian woodlands. Wild lands are being paved over and plowed under at a furious rate. Experts estimate that one million to two million more acres will be developed by 2005 to accommodate the nearly 2,000 people added to the state's population every day.

The environmental impact of California's burgeoning population appears in the air people breathe and the water they drink. Although Los Angeles is world-renowned for its smoggy skies, 8 other air-quality regions in the state are also among the country's 20 dirtiest. Water pollution is an ongoing problem too. The Sacramento–San Joaquin Delta provides 20 million people in the drought-plagued state with fresh water, but its quality has been seriously threatened by poisonous runoff from farms, housing tracts, and cities.

Environmental degradation and loss of habitat have had an even greater effect on the state's native wildlife. As Californians joke that their earthquake-prone state is sliding into the ocean, their wildlife is sliding inexorably toward extinction. Although extinction has always been a natural process in California—as exemplified by the remains of pygmy mammoths on Santa Cruz Island and giant seagoing lizards in the Coast Range—the rate of extinction since the 1849 gold rush has been decidedly unnatural.

No fewer than 20 animal and 35 plant species have been pushed over the edge of oblivion in the past 150 years, notable among them the gray wolf, long-eared kit fox, Santa Barbara song sparrow, and Xerces blue butterfly. These days the only place in California to see a native grizzly bear is on the state flag. Jaguars, bison, and white-tailed deer no longer roam here, nor do 8 species of native freshwater fish still swim in the state.

That 12 more species of native fish are in danger of following suit indicates an alarming trend: The number of species in trouble in California is growing. At last count, 280 plant and animal species and subspecies had

ABOVE: *A captive breeding program is now reintroducing the California condor, the rarest and largest North American land bird, to the wilds.*

been listed under the California Endangered Species Act as in danger of extinction or elimination within the state's borders. Among them are 25 species of birds, including 2 indelibly linked to the state's image, the California condor and the California brown pelican. Biologists have identified another 60 animal species and 600 plants that meet the state's criteria for listing, and as the human population grows, these numbers will no doubt increase.

Fortunately for California's wildlife, great efforts are underway to preserve and protect remaining habitat. Despite its urbanization, industrialization, and agricultural conversion, California retains large chunks of natural habitat, mostly in its public lands. Nearly half of California is owned and managed by government agencies. Twenty million acres, one fifth of the state, fall within 17 national forests. Another 4.5 million acres are included in 6 different national parks and 12 national monuments and national recreation areas. Increasing the total are 24 national wildlife refuge complexes, hundreds of state and county parks, dozens of private preserves, and huge military reserves.

In these areas visitors can still find natural California. To make exploration and enjoyment easier, this book divides the state into four distinct regions, defined as much by proximity as by biogeography. The first is the California desert, the 25-million-acre southeastern corner of the state that encompasses three distinct deserts—the Sonoran, Mojave, and Great Basin—and contains a bounty of biological wonders as well as dramatic geology and spectacular landscapes.

The second is the state's magnificent backbone, the soaring granitic peaks of the Sierra Nevada, which features 500 summits over 12,000 feet, as well as 8 national forests, 3 national parks, 14 wilderness areas, and dozens of state parks and monuments. Within them live hundreds of fascinating species, including the oldest and the largest living trees in the world.

The third region is little-known northern California. Unparalleled in biodiversity, it contains the lush Sacramento Valley, rugged mountain ranges, still-active volcanoes, vast lava fields, windswept sagebrush and chaparral plateaus, dense oak woodlands, huge lakes teeming with migratory waterfowl, wild and scenic rivers, towering coast redwood forests, and an inspiring coastline.

Among the highlights of the fourth area, the scenic California coast, are coast redwood forests, saline marshes, intertidal zones, and coastal dunes. Living in these regions are a great number of wildlife species, from lumbering marine mammals such as the elephant seal to tiny coastal wildflowers such as the endangered Menzies wallflower.

In exploring these areas of natural California, visitors discover its true wealth: a myriad of plants and animals living in a complex web of ecosystems that become more valuable with each passing day.

RIGHT *In the High Sierra's Ansel Adams Wilderness, Banner Peak and Mount Ritter, imposing and granite gray, overlook tiny jewel-like alpine lakes. White and pink mountain heathers cover the slopes.*

THE CALIFORNIA DESERT

eserts are like dreams. Scenes there unfold in stark monochromes. Actions seem disconnected, distances deceiving, dimensions distorted. Winds push boulders across dry lake beds. Tantalizing pools of water float on the horizon, ever so realistic, ever out of reach. Mountains materialize at dawn, then melt into the sky at night. A sand dune mimics a drift of snow. When they do appear, colors come in bright, haphazard bursts. Like the blooms of desert wildflowers after a rain, they are as ephemeral as last night's slumberous wanderings.

Although it encompasses many ecotypes, California is above all a land with a desert heart. Rain—or more accurately, the lack of it—is the defining element for the state's biogeography. Rainfall of less than 5 inches annually makes the 25 million acres in the state's southeastern quarter three different deserts: the Sonoran, Mojave, and Great Basin.

Although all are arid, the three deserts differ in geographic and biological features. No single road links them. In the south is the Sonoran, the northern reach of a huge desert that stretches across the international border from its namesake state in northwestern Mexico. Nicknamed the Colorado Desert in California for the river that forms the state's eastern boundary, the Sonoran is considered "low" desert in

LEFT: *Dotted by hardy desert shrubs and feathery grasses, undulating sand dunes ebb and flow across Death Valley National Park. Fierce winds create the riblike designs that pattern the rolling, arid terrain.*

topographic terms because it is distinguished by lower elevations, hotter temperatures, and less rainfall. Vegetatively, the Sonoran boasts flatlands covered with creosote bush, sandy washes lined with mesquite, paloverde, and smoke trees, and more kinds of cactus than its northern neighbors. Spidery ocotillo—whose red-tipped blossoms resemble tubes of lipstick before they unfurl each morning—grows on rocky slopes, and California fan palm shades cool oases.

As it extends northward, the Sonoran gives way to the Mojave Desert along an imaginary line running west to east at approximately the same latitude as downtown Los Angeles. A 15,000-square-mile patch of rugged mountain ranges, dry lake beds, and shimmering alkali flats that spills into southern Nevada, the Mojave is labeled "high" desert because it contains tall mountain ranges as well as its generally high elevation. That classification seems at odds with the elevation marker in nearby Death Valley's Badwater Basin, which claims 282 feet below sea level, the lowest point in the Western Hemisphere. Although much of its land is covered by the creosote-bush and bur-sage vegetation community of its southern neighbor, the Mojave is easily identified by the spiky leaves of its two most distinctive residents, the prehistoric Joshua tree and its smaller cousin, the Mojave yucca.

Farther north is California's third and smallest desert, the westernmost edge of the Great Basin Desert, an arid washboard of alternating basin and range that is more closely associated with Nevada and Utah than the Golden State. Occupying a narrow sliver of land wedged between the towering granite walls of the Sierra Nevada on the west and the state's eastern boundary, California's Great Basin Desert is little known and seldom visited. Sagebrush and juniper-pinyon woodland are its vegetative hallmarks; its climatological signature is colder and wetter winters, when snow on the purple-green sea of sagebrush looks like an ocean frothing with wind-whipped whitecaps.

Far from lifeless, California's deserts teem with an amazing array of unique wildlife. In spring, lush thickets of honey mesquite and flowering brittlebush attract hundreds of species of birds. Desert natives such as

OVERLEAF: *For a few weeks each spring, the blossoms of magenta hedgehog cactus, yellow brittlebush, and other flowering plants at Anza-Borrego Desert State Park splash Yaqui Flat with color.*

THE
DESERT

25 Miles
25 Kilometers

NEVADA

95

15

DEATH
VALLEY
NATIONAL
MONUMENT

Cottonwood Mtns

395

190 Telescope
Peak   x
Panamint Range

190

Coffin Pk

Funeral
Peak

Amargosa Range

Death Valley

Black Mtns

Amargosa River

Tecopa

AMARGOSA CANYON
NATURAL AREA

China
Lake

Searles
Lake

PINNACLES NAT
NATURAL LANDMARK

127

15

Granite Range

AUDUBON
WILDLIFE
SANCTUARY AT
BUTTERBREDT SPRING

RED ROCK
CANYON
TATE PARK

DESERT
TORTOISE
NATURAL AREA

California
City

395

MOJAVE

Baker

15

Ivanpah Range

New York Range

EAST MOJAVE
NAT SCENIC
AREA

Pinto Range

MOJAVE
CINDER CONES
NAT NATURAL
LANDMARK

Providence Rge

PROVIDENCE MTNS
STATE REC AREA

MITCHELL CAVERNS

Sacramento Mtns

ANTELOPE
VALLEY
CALIFORNIA POPPY
RESERVE

SADDLEBACK
BUTTE SP

Lancaster

x
Saddleback
Butte

Mojave River

DESERT

KELSO DUNES
Granite
Mtns

Bristol Mtns

95

San Andreas

San Gabriel Mtns

210

Transverse

Fault

Range

Bullion Mountains

AMBOY CRATER
NAT NATURAL
LANDMARK

Amboy

Bristol
Lake

5

15

BIG MORONGO
PRESERVE

62

Twentynine
Palms

Pinto Mtns

Coxcomb Mtns

62

10

Palm Springs

215

Little San Bernardino Mtns

JOSHUA TREE NATL
MON

Eagle Mtns

95

Thousand
Palms

COACHELLA
VALLEY
PRESERVE

79

Coachella Valley

86

Santa Rosa Mtns

Salton Sea

SALTON SEA STATE
RECREATION AREA

SONORAN

10

5

PACIFIC OCEAN

CALIFORNIA
PAINTED
DESERT

ANZA
BORREGO
SP

78

SALTON SEA
NATL WILDLIFE
REFUGE

DESERT

Colorado

78

15

Salton

Trough

8

San Diego

8

8

MEXICO

phainopeplas, cactus wrens, and roadrunners are visited by exotic migrants like Tennessee warblers, red-eyed vireos, and vermilion flycatchers, while California gulls nest beside desert lakes hundreds of miles inland. Desert kit foxes no bigger than house cats prey on giant kangaroo rats. Bighorn sheep cling to craggy mountaintops. To escape their predators, specially adapted lizards that have evolved over millions of years "swim" beneath sand dunes. Desert tortoises, whose genetic profile dates back to Pleistocene times, lumber across the Mojave, and ancient pupfish swim in underground waters released by earthquake faults.

In this land of antiquity, little has changed over the past million years, except perhaps our opinion of it. Most of the settlers who trekked across it in the 1800s shared the feeling of the U.S. topographical engineer Lieutenant Joseph C. Ives. After an early reconnaissance, he reported back to Washington, D.C., that the region "is, of course, altogether valueless. After entering it there is nothing to do but leave. Ours had been the first, and will doubtless be the last, party of whites to visit this profitless locality." Today millions of visitors come each year—900,000 to Death Valley National Monument alone—to enjoy the dramatic vistas, otherworldly scenery, and flora and fauna galore. Perhaps most of all, visitors seek increasingly valuable commodities: wide-open spaces, clear skies, fresh air, and the peace and tranquillity only the desert can provide.

This chapter's circular exploration of California's deserts begins in the Sonoran Desert, in the southeastern corner of the state at Anza-Borrego Desert State Park. It continues east to the Salton Sea, then north into the East Mojave Desert and Joshua Tree National Park. Heading northeast, it visits the Mojave cinder cones and the Providence Mountains, then turns north to Death Valley National Monument in the West Mojave Desert. The return trip west and south includes stops at the Desert Tortoise Natural Area and the Antelope Valley poppy preserve, near the city of Lancaster. When traveling in the desert, schedule driving time for midday, when the heat makes hiking difficult, and be sure to have a supply of water and sunscreen and a vehicle in good working order.

ANZA-BORREGO AND COACHELLA VALLEY

Shaded on a map, California's Sonoran Desert resembles a large bite taken out of the state's southeast corner. Visitors here, however, find a

ABOVE: *Fast and fearless, the greater roadrunner, a crested cuckoo, rarely takes flight; it relies instead on long, sturdy legs to run down desert-dwelling prey including lizards, birds, and rattlesnakes.*

feast, not a famine, of biological riches. From San Diego take Interstate 8 east and Route 79 north to Route 78, which runs through the middle of this varied and colorful desert and just 70 miles east of downtown San Diego reaches its most spectacular section, 600,000-acre **Anza-Borrego Desert State Park❖.** Established in 1933, the park takes its name from early explorer Juan Bautista de Anza—who passed through in 1774 seeking a land route between Sonora, Mexico, and the Spanish missions along the California coast—and from the rare desert bighorn sheep that live here (*borrego* is Spanish for sheep). Much of the desert looks as it did when de Anza first saw it. Groves of fan palms (the largest palms in North America) screen improbable oases as an unrelenting sun bakes desolate badlands into shades ranging from pink to chocolate. Pinyon pines sprout atop jagged mountains while cacti speckle the broad desert plains. Mountain lions and coyotes live alongside leopard lizards and chuckwallas.

The park owes its biological diversity to its unique geographic setting. Sandwiched between the tall peaks of the Peninsular ranges (the Santa Ana, San Jacinto, and Santa Rosa mountain chains) to the west

ABOVE: *Century plants such as these at Anza-Borrego may require years to flower—but not 100 as their name suggests. Native Americans made these and other agaves into food, liquor, and medicines.*

and the dry, low-lying Salton Trough to the east, Anza-Borrego is a land of climatic extremes. Temperatures fluctuate wildly, from 0 degrees Fahrenheit in winter in the high country to 120 degrees in summer in the low desert. In the high country along the park's western boundary rain can average 20 to 30 inches a year, but just a few miles east only 2 to 3 inches fall. Although most of the precipitation occurs in winter, tropical storms occasionally blow in from Mexico during the summer, dumping several inches of rain at a time and unleashing flash floods that can reshape the landscape in an instant.

In spring, the rains can ignite an explosion of color. The otherwise brown and green scrubby floor of the Borrego Valley turns as bright as an Oriental carpet when purple sand verbena, white dune evening

24

primroses, and yellow desert sunflowers weave a multicolored pattern with their blossoms. Look for yellow ghost flowers, pink Bigelow monkeyflowers, and purple Arizona lupines in the rocky washes that twist and turn through the park.

All those flowering plants attract plenty of wildlife—thousands of species of insects, 250 species of birds, 60 reptiles, and 60 mammals. A good place to view them is Borrego Palm Canyon, one of 25 canyons in the park where the most significant groves of fan palms grow. From Route 78, take Route S22, Palm Canyon Drive, to the not-to-be-missed visitor center, a part-subterranean structure designed to blend into the desert. Nearby, a 1.5-mile trail follows Palm Canyon Creek through a natural garden of ocotillo (Native Americans made a lemonade-like beverage from its tart blossoms), aptly named cheesebush (rub the stem and smell to learn why), and yellow-flowered brittlebush (Spanish padres used its aromatic resin as incense).

A thousand years ago, boulders along the trail were hollowed out and used as grinding slicks by Cahuilla Indians. The canyon walls, where peninsular bighorn sheep (one of three subspecies of bighorn in the state) pick their surefooted way, are painted with desert varnish, a dark-brown patina created by bacteria and chemical reactions between the rock and environment. The trail

ABOVE: *After spring rains, the spidery limbs of the ocotillo sprout tubular red blossoms at the tip of each spiny branch.*
BELOW: *Known as* tunas *in Spanish, the fruit of the prickly pear cactus is edible.*

25

ends at a series of deep pools screened by 800 California fan palms, which can grow to 50 feet. The skirt of dead leaves, or fronds, completely obscures the trunks of some, giving them the look of shaggy musk oxen. The dense honey mesquite thickets crowding the creek's banks attract plenty of birds, including Anna's and Costa's hummingbirds. Of the two, Anna's are the bigger; their throat patches, called gorgets, are red, and Costa's are deep violet. Along the water- and wind-polished boulders that line this cool and peaceful oasis, cactus wrens, largest in the wren family, spread their tail feathers as coquettishly as Spanish fan dancers.

Head east through the park on County Road S22 (then south on Route 86) along the old Truckhaven Trail, where the towering Santa Rosa Mountains rise to the north and the Borrego Badlands sprawl to the south. The Santa Rosas, which have emerged during the last three million to four million years, show their youth in precipitous slopes, minimal vegetation, and picture-perfect alluvial fans (fan-shaped de-posits laid down by a branching stream). The blacktop leads through the **Mecca Hills❖**, where the corrugated landscape of the **Painted Canyon** looks and feels like a tie-dyed miniature Grand Canyon.

The heavily eroded arroyos flatten out into the Salton Trough, an ancient seabed that was once the northern extension of the Gulf of California. Gradually, silt deposits from the Colorado River formed a natural dam, blocking the gulf and creating an ancient sea. Over time, the sea evaporated, leaving a dry alkaline basin. In 1905, when an irri-gation canal used to divert waters from the Colorado for agricultural development failed, the river flowed unchecked into the basin for two years, producing today's **Salton Sea.** Fed by agricultural drainage and runoff, it covers upward of 380 square miles and lies more than 200 feet below sea level.

At the south end, off Route 86, is the **Salton Sea National Wildlife Refuge❖.** Open water, salt marshes, freshwater ponds, and desert scrub in the refuge's 2,200 acres support 400 bird species, including during the winter tens of thousands of waterfowl and shorebirds such as Canada geese, snow geese, American avocets, black-necked stilts, pintail, green-winged teal, and eared grebes. South American species—flamingos, brown boobies, and frigate birds—have also found their way here. Endangered Yuma clapper rails breed in mature cattail-bul-rush stands in shallow water, and threatened bald eagles, endangered

ABOVE: *Great blue herons congregate in a crowded treetop rookery in the Salton Sea National Wildlife Refuge. More than 400 bird species use the area's open waters, salt marshes, and freshwater ponds.*

California brown pelicans, and endangered peregrine falcons also visit. Although the area is extremely hot in summer, intrepid birders find yellow-footed gulls, black skimmers, wood storks, and fulvous whistling ducks. Occupying 18 miles of the northeast shore of the sea is the **Salton Sea Recreation Area❖,** reached by Route 111, which follows the east shore. Bird-watching is good here too, but the principal attraction is saltwater sport fishing. The sea has been heavily stocked with sargos, gulf croakers, and orangemouth corbinas, oceangoing fish native to the Gulf of California that were introduced during the 1950s.

Continue north of the Salton Sea on Route 86 and Interstate 10 through the fertile Coachella Valley, home to date palms, citrus groves, grapevines, subdivisions, and golf courses. Although Palm Springs and its environs have become the most famous feature in the valley, relics of the region's natural past hold fast in a nearly 20,000-acre patch of sand dunes and hidden palm oases near Thousand Palms just off I-10, the **Coachella Valley Preserve❖.**

Jointly owned and managed by the Bureau of Land Management, U.S. Fish and Wildlife Service, California departments of Fish and Game and Parks and Recreation, and the Nature Conservancy, Coachella Valley boasts one of the largest and most breathtaking groves of native California fan palms in the Southwest. Here, in the shade of rustling fronds, pools of crystal-clear water freed by earthquake faults bubble up. Within the preserve's boundaries, eleven oases support 1,200 native *Washington filifera,* the second-largest concentration of native palms in the state. Fed by continuously flowing springs along the San Andreas fault, the shady waters have offered humans relief from the harsh desert sands for more than 600 years. The Cahuilla Indians found shelter here, gathering edibles from mesquite, agave, and yucca and hunting resident bighorn sheep, blacktailed mule deer, pronghorn, rodents, and rabbits. Later, trappers, prospectors, and homesteaders came.

ABOVE: *A desert denizen, the male Costa's hummingbird perches conspicuously on a stump to claim his territory.*

RIGHT: *In the arid desert near Palm Springs, thousands of large water-loving fan palms thrive in Palm Canyon, a moist, tree-shaded oasis.*

The oases are surrounded by sand dunes. In this spartan habitat, where on summer days the surface sizzles at temperatures reaching 180 degrees, protective rocks and shading shrubs are as rare as redwoods in the Sahara, and rain seldom falls. The dunes' most notable resident is the threatened Coachella Valley fringe-toed lizard. A marvel of adaptation, the eight-to-ten-inch-long lizard can submerge and literally swim through the sand to escape not only the searing heat but also such formidable predators as greater roadrunners, whipsnakes, burrowing owls, and loggerhead shrikes.

Take the self-guided interpretative trail, an easy mile-long loop that begins at the visitor center and winds through the lush groves and along a chain of pools that gleam like pearls. Look closely in the water for schools of desert pupfish, and watch for birds feeding in the brittlebush, smoke trees, and creosote bushes. Plan to visit in spring,

fall, or winter as summer air temperatures reach a blood-boiling 120 degrees. Wildlife viewing is best at dawn and dusk, when animals are most active and the desert sun brushes the sky with colors, a changing palette reflected in the ocher-tinged Indio Hills.

North of Thousand Palms and Palm Springs, turn northeast off I-10 on Route 62 to **Big Morongo Preserve❖**. Etched into the northwestern flank of the Little San Bernadino Mountains, Big Morongo Canyon was formed during a series of events lasting thousands of years, when a plateau with two rivers running across it from north to south dropped and became an abyss. The down-faulting generated so much friction and heat that the walls of the abyss were sealed and became impervious to water. Some of the oldest rocks in California are exposed in the canyon, where the heat and pressure transformed two-billion-year-old granite into gneiss and schist.

The year-round water of the verdant oasis in Big Morongo, among the ten largest natural desert oases in the state, nourishes one of the five largest tracts of southern cottonwood-willow riparian forest in the California desert outside the Colorado River. Within the preserve's boundaries are five distinct plant communities containing at least 355 different types of plants. A display of pressed specimens is on view in a small trailer near the preserve manager's cabin. Creosote-bush scrub covers the hills and ridge tops above the creek; below, Mojave yucca, catclaw, Mormon tea, and various cacti species supply cover for such mammals as coyotes, black-tailed hares, and antelope ground squirrels. Loggerhead shrikes prey on side-blotched lizards, Gilbert's skinks, and yucca night lizards, while coveys of Gambel's quail scurry through indigo bush and brittlebush. Mockingbirds and scrub jays shriek from California juniper.

No fewer than 270 species of birds have been spotted in this narrow six-mile-long desert canyon, including such rarities as least Bell's vireos, vermilion flycatchers, black-chinned sparrows, dusky flycatchers, black-throated gray warblers, Tennessee warblers, red-eyed vireos, American redstarts, and ovenbirds. Compared with other desert study areas, Big Morongo boasts three times the number of bird species.

The preserve owes its diverse birdlife to its location in a transition zone between the Mojave Desert, the Sonoran Desert, and the coast, an unusual blend of environments allowing flora and fauna from all three habitats to coexist. The mélange attracts strange bedfellows:

Where else does a coast-loving Nuttall's woodpecker nest side by side with a desert-dwelling ladder-backed woodpecker?

The Morongo fault forces groundwater to the surface in a series of springs, creating more than 20 acres of wetland that supports a community of freshwater marsh plants: cattails, Olney bulrushes, yerba mansa, and watercress. Marsh wrens, Virginia rails, song sparrows, and yellowthroats feed and nest in this habitat. As the water accumulates, it forms a stream that sustains two or three miles of a healthy corridor of riparian woodland. The grove of Fremont cottonwoods, red willows, and slender willows provides nesting sites for Bewick's wrens, common bushtits, Cooper's hawks, and great horned owls. Gray foxes, raccoons, and ringtails are also riparian residents. Buckthorn cholla, desert catalpa, and desert mistletoe grow in the desert wash, where diamondback rattlesnakes lie in wait for Merriam's kangaroo rats and long-tailed pocket mice. Verdins, phainopeplas, and cactus wrens flit among the honey mesquite. The creek then becomes an open desert watercourse for four more miles.

For centuries, Big Morongo Canyon provided nomadic Native Americans with an easy route between high and low deserts. The oasis at the canyon's mouth served as an ideal campsite because water was available, game was plentiful, and sheltering caves lay nearby. Among the artifacts uncovered in archaeological sites here are fire rings, pottery shards, and grinding slicks and mortar holes.

Connecting nature trails loop through the preserve (several boardwalk paths can accommodate wheelchairs). The popular Cottonwood Trail leads from the information kiosk near the parking lot to the heart of the oasis, where a strategically placed viewing platform overlooks the freshwater marsh and eight-foot cattails form a natural blind for visitors scanning for birds. From the Cottonwood Trail, take the Willow Trail, which follows the creek as it winds beneath multitiered greenery. Along the trail, guaranteed to strain visitors' necks, a symphony of birdsong beckons from overhanging branches. Don't forget to look down to spot soras and Virginia rails—even rare black rails—feeding among the marsh plants.

JOSHUA TREE NATIONAL PARK

To enter the Mojave Desert proper, continue east on Route 62 over the Little San Bernadino Mountains. The Mojave River divides East and

West Mojave, two halves that are noticeably different topographically. Except for the Panamint and Amargosa ranges at Death Valley, part of the Great Basin Desert, the western Mojave is typically flat, whereas the eastern is much more mountainous. In this land of extremes—sizzling in summer, freezing in winter—where there is little shade from the sun and no shelter from the wind, nature's power is quiet, palpable, absolute. One of the most forbidding places on earth, the Mojave can also be incredibly enchanting, especially in March, April, and May, when winter rains have set wildflowers blazing across the scrub-studded flats and rolling hills. The fringes of leaves on the Joshua trees rustle like a hula dancer's grass skirt, and migrant songbirds splash the gray-green creosote-bush landscape with feathery red, blue, and yellow.

At the town of Twentynine Palms lies the entrance to **Joshua Tree National Park❖,** a 734,000-acre desert sanctuary originally set aside as a national monument in 1936 to preserve scenic portions of both the Mojave and Colorado deserts. In 1994, it gained full national-park status. To learn why it deserves that protection, stop at the visitor center and watch a fascinating slide show that captures the magic and mystery of this unique habitat. Behind park headquarters, a half-mile self-guided nature trail loops around the Oasis of Mara, which means "the place of little springs and much grass" in the language of the Serrano, Native Americans who gathered here for thousands of years, eating the flowers and fruit of the California fan palm and making baskets, hats, and sandals from its leaves. The willow and fig trees that now grow here are the legacy of European settlers who arrived following the discovery of gold in 1873. Look for hooded and northern (or Bullock's) orioles, brown towhees, and Lincoln's and song sparrows in the thickets of mesquite that thrive at the base of the fan palms.

A 40-mile driving tour circles from the visitor center through the park's most scenic areas. Of the numerous signed pullouts dotting the route, most feature short self-guided nature loops. In the Mojave Desert portion of the park, the Joshua tree reigns supreme. Called "the most repulsive tree in the vegetable Kingdom" by early California explorer John C. Frémont, this hardy woody perennial belongs to the agave family. To the Mormon pioneers trekking across the Mojave Desert from Salt Lake City who named it, the limbs of the giant yucca tree resembled the up-stretched arms of Joshua beckoning them to the promised land. In a

ABOVE: *The largest of the yuccas, the Joshua tree is a desert-dwelling evergreen whose spiny, daggerlike leaves once fed the extinct giant sloth; its flowers and pods now support some 25 bird species.*

lifetime that often spans centuries, the spiky tree can grow to a height of more than 30 feet. One of the largest and possibly oldest ones at the park is the 900-year-old, 31.8-foot giant at upper Covington Flat.

The Joshua tree is the focal point for a complex community of wildlife. Cactus wrens hop around the branches feeding on the numerous insects that infest the tree. Yellow and black Scott's orioles hang their sacklike nests from the limbs, and fallen branches provide a home for desert wood rats and yucca night lizards, which feed on termites. The Joshua tree owes its existence to the tiny hyperactive yucca moth, which flits from tree to tree collecting nectar from the creamy white flowers in spring. The female rolls the pollen into a ball and forces it down the flower of another tree to provide a source of food

33

for her young when they hatch from the eggs she lays there. In the process, she pollinates the tree.

Beneath the Joshua trees grow a profusion of desert plants and wildflowers whose blooms create a spring kaleidoscope of color. Yellow blossoms appear on desert trumpet, coreopsis, chinchweed, and tansy mustard. Desert tortoises munch on the yellow petals of desert dandelions, and antelope squirrels feast on the leaves of the yellow-blossomed fiddleneck. Pink and purple flowers are fringed amaranth, filaree, locoweed, desert calico, and Mojave aster. Red and orange blossoms include desert paintbrush, desert mariposa, and desert mallow. Lupines, desert gilias, amsonias, and Canterbury bells bloom blue, and white is the color of California primroses, wishbones, sand blazing stars, and tidytips.

Geology is readily apparent throughout the drive. The park is on the eastern end of the broad mountainous belt called the Transverse Range because it runs west to east rather than north to south like most of California's mountain chains. Several distinct ranges cross the park: the Little San Bernadinos in the southwestern part, the Cottonwood, Hexie, and Pinto mountains in the center, and the Eagle and Coxcomb mountains in the eastern part. Steep escarpments rising abruptly from the lower desert areas mark the north and south margins of the park, and much of the land within its boundaries lies above 4,000 feet. The valleys between were carved by erosion or formed by down-dropping along faults, called grabens.

The dark formation of metamorphic rock is pinto gneiss, a composition of quartz, feldspar, and biotite dating back a billion years. About 100 million years ago, a younger, lighter-colored mass of monzonite rose to the surface and intruded the pinto gneiss. Uplifting, down-dropping, and horizontal slipping of crustal blocks along the hundreds of faults that run through the park, together with erosion from wind and rain, have created a wonderland of geologic structures. An eroded volcanic dome rises in southern Queen Valley. Multicolored basalt columns in the Lost Horse Mountains are stacked one atop another like layers of meat, bread, and cheese in a cartoon sandwich

LEFT: *Although it tolerates temperatures up to 115 degrees, the desert iguana climbs into bushes or cacti such as this blossoming prickly pear for a breath of cooler air when the land surface gets too hot.*

crafted by Dagwood Bumstead. Inselbergs (isolated mountains) of quartz monzonite at Hidden Valley Campground resemble giant haystacks, and at Jumbo Rocks, spheroidal weathering has left boulders looking like gigantic skulls and other recognizable shapes.

EAST MOJAVE

When the loop ends on Route 62, return to Twentynine Palms and take Amboy Road north between the Bullion and Sheep Hole mountains and across Bristol Lake, a desert playa encrusted with salt that looks as otherworldly as the surface of the moon. Outside the blink-and-miss-it hamlet of Amboy rises **Amboy Crater National Natural Landmark❖,** a 200-foot-high blackened cinder cone surrounded by miles of asphaltlike lava beds. After a half-hour walk across the lava to the base of this relatively new volcano, hikers can reach the unusually flat crater floor by walking around to the west side, where a lava flow has breached the wall.

Five miles east of Amboy on old Route 66, head north on Kelbaker Road, which leads between the Bristol and Marble mountains and across Interstate 40 into the 1.4-million-acre **Mojave National Preserve❖.** Bounded by Interstate 15 to the north and Route 95 to the east, this isolated wedge of Mojave Desert is commonly and deservedly called the Lonesome Triangle. Although larger than the state of Delaware, the official scenic area is home to only a handful of people.

Often called a desert of mountains, the East Mojave is cross-hatched by ranges. The Granite, Providence, Mid Hill, and New York ranges trend southwest to northeast while the Sacramento, Bristol, and Old Dad mountains run southeast to northwest. Completing the picture are the north-south Piute and Ivanpah ranges. At the base of these highly eroded granitic ranges, apron-shaped alluvial fans have formed from a buildup of loose sedimentary rocks washed down from the slopes. Fans that coalesce at a mountain front are called *bajadas.*

The land between the ranges is fascinating. Kelbaker Road skirts the 45-square-mile exquisitely sculpted **Kelso Dunes,** which are among the most extensive in the Western Hemisphere. Some are as

---

RIGHT: *In the East Mojave desert, a creosote bush basks in the fading afterglow of evening as a full moon climbs high above the fragile Kelso Dunes. The limestone peaks of the Providence Mountains rise beyond.*

tall as a seven-story building. Hikers can hear the dunes boom, mystifying sounds made by polished grains of rose quartz sliding over the underlying surface. More than 100 species of plants grow here, including sand verbena, desert primrose, mesquite, and the ubiquitous creosote bush. Among the most unusual residents of the dunes is the Kelso Dune Jerusalem cricket, which lives nowhere else in the world.

At the **Providence Mountains State Recreation Area❖,** the region's tallest mountains—limestone peaks intermixed with ancient volcanic, sedimentary, and crystalline rock—rise dramatically 6,000 to 7,000 feet above the desert floor. The upper slopes are dotted with juniper and pinyon pine, and bighorn sheep roam the higher elevations. Views from the top are breathtaking, as are the ones inside the mountains. At **Mitchell Caverns,** ranger-led tours explore two subterranean chambers where calcite deposits have created a gorgeous display of stalactites, stalagmites, flowstone, cave spaghetti, cave shields, and cave ribbons. Outside the entrance to the caverns are a small campground and a self-guided nature-study trail, named for longtime Mojave botanist Mary Beal, that loops through stands of catclaw, creosote bush, buckthorn cholla, and prickly pear.

Volcanoes have also left their mark on the eastern Mojave. Kelbaker Road continues through the 25,600 acres of lava fields and cinder cones. Of the 32 cinder cones found here, some were formed in recent geologic time—within the last 1,000 years—and others date back nearly 10 million years. The red and black cones rise 300 feet above white sandy washes and fields of black lava and display a wide range of volcanic structures—collapsed lava tubes and many types of cones. Other examples of vulcanism in the region include a 75-square-mile uplift of once-molten rock known as **Cima Dome** (covered by one of the thickest stands of Joshua trees in the Mojave) and a range of jagged red spires, **Castle Peaks.**

DEATH VALLEY NATIONAL PARK
At the town of Baker, Kelbaker Road leaves the scenic area, crosses Interstate 15, and becomes Route 127 as it enters the West Mojave. Follow it through 48 miles of unrelenting, unpopulated creosote scrub to the Spanish Trail Highway east to Tecopa and south along a dirt road to **Amargosa Canyon Natural Area❖.** The Amargosa River

(which means bitter water in Spanish) flows through 9,500 acres jointly owned by the State Land Commission and the U.S. Bureau of Land
Management. The year-round water winds through deeply eroded
badlands and canyons, its lush pools and wetlands surrounded by
willows and cottonwoods. The trees attract blue grosbeaks, willow flycatchers, northern pygmy owls, and two endangered species, the least
Bell's vireo and western yellow-billed cuckoo. The cuckoo nests only
in willows, timing its egg laying to coincide with the hatching of the
area's most common insects, caterpillars and katydids. Ruddy ducks
and teal join great blue herons, sandpipers, and Canada geese in
seeking the secluded ponds created by the river, whose clear water
supports Amargosa pupfish and Nevada speckled dace. One mile up-
river from Tecopa is **Grimshaw Lake Natural Area❖,** where white-
fronted geese rest during their spring and fall migrations. The area is
also home to the endangered Amargosa vole, a tiny cinnamon-colored
rodent that requires wetland habitat to survive and travels no more
than 400 feet from its birthplace during its lifetime. South of the
canyon are the **Dumont Dunes,** a small but scenic field of blow-sand
that shifts with the wind because no vegetation holds it down.

Back on Route 127 north, turn west onto Route 178 just beyond
Shoshone to reach the southern entrance of the most famous and
popular desert park in the country, **Death Valley National Park❖.**
Death Valley occupies 2.3 million acres of some of the hottest, driest,
most forbidding—and most beautiful—landscape on earth. Snow-
dusted peaks 11,000 feet high overlook a dazzling white salt pan 282
feet below sea level. Against a backdrop of variegated rock formations, sand dunes like those found in the Sahara shift and snake.
Layers of rock exposed by wind and rain and heat look like a
Neapolitan ice-cream bar. Desert pupfish swim in 111-degree water
five times saltier than the ocean, and delicate spring wildflowers
sprout from ground as hard and sun-dried as an adobe brick.

Powerful geologic forces shaped and painted Death Valley. During
the past three million years, two mountain ranges—the nearly two-

---

OVERLEAF: *From Death Valley National Park's aptly named Dantes View,
barren salt flats, heat-racked alluvial fans, and tormented escarpments vividly call to mind the Italian poet's description of purgatory.*

ABOVE: *Seared and scarred, the walls of Little Ubehebe Crater are dramatic testaments to Death Valley's violent past. Here dark volcanic cinders sit atop lighter-colored—and older—alluvial fan rocks.*

mile-high Panamint Range to the west and the Black Mountains to the east—rose violently upward while the earth's crust between them slumped below sea level. Next nature's sculpting tools went to work. Alternating sun and ice splintered the exposed rock, and rain swept away the looser pieces, blunting the peaks and carving deep furrows into their sides, exposing the very innards of earth. To the north, glaciers came and went, creating huge rivers of meltwater and filling the valley with ephemeral lakes. When the climate became hotter and drier, leaving Death Valley in the enormous rain shadow of the Sierra Nevada, lakes evaporated and streams dried up. Today Death Valley receives less than two inches of rain per year. In summer, daytime temperatures routinely soar to a skin-blistering 120 degrees.

Early visitors encountering the furnacelike blast of heat thought they had ventured into Hell, and one look at the area's raw topography confirmed the impression. The lifeless salt flats, fiery red escarpments, and tortuous canyons suggest the underworld as surely as the place names reflect it. Besides Death Valley, there are Hells Gate, Coffin Peak, Funeral Peak, and Dantes View, an overlook in the Black Mountains inspired by the famed poet's description of purgatory. Devils Golf Course is a mile of rock-salt spikes carved by rain from the crusty residue of a former lake. Forty miles north is Devils Cornfield.

ABOVE: *Death Valley's Zabriskie Point is surrounded by rolling mud-stone badlands that support little vegetation. The Gibraltar-like cliff was thrust up by geologic collisions and sculpted by wind and rain.*

Death Valley is far from lifeless, however. Of the more than a thousand kinds of flowering plants that live here—including ferns, lilies, and orchids—most are specially adapted to the harsh environment. Mesquite sends its taproots down a hundred feet in search of water, and desert holly coats its leaves with salt to diffuse the sunlight. Other plants have skins allowing very little evaporation. Wildlife is also abundant. Close to 400 species breed here, including 290 bird species, 57 mammals, 36 reptiles, 3 amphibians, and 5 species of pupfish. To deal with temperature extremes, most animals are nocturnal, taking advantage of the night coolness. The kangaroo rat lives all its life without taking a single sip of water because it metabolizes its food to obtain the liquid it needs. The sidewinder rattlesnake avoids the midday heat by burying itself up to its nose, and when it must travel, it continuously loops its body to avoid absorbing heat from the ground. Desert bighorn survive by frequenting the forests of juniper, pinyon, bristlecone pine, and mountain mahogany on the cooler, higher peaks. If forced to, they can go several days without drinking. One of the few desert creatures seemingly unperturbed by the heat is the roadrunner, a member of the cuckoo family, which in winter stands with its back to the sun so that its dark feathers absorb heat.

October through May is the best time to visit the park. Death

43

Valley's size and the distances separating its major features make driving essential. Route 178 leads north to **Badwater Basin,** the lowest, driest point in the United States, and a couple of miles farther north, a one-way loop called Artists Drive passes **Artists Palette,** a multicolored hillside painted red, yellow, orange, green, violet, brown, and black by oxidation of iron, magnesium, and other minerals. At sunrise or sunset, the interpretative trail at Golden Canyon shows visitors where this rumpled gorge gets its name.

When Route 178 dead-ends into Route 190, to the east is **Zabriskie Point,** the most all-encompassing viewpoint in the park, and to the north and west is the oasis at Furnace Creek, a good spot to see great-tailed grackles, Wilson's warblers, and white-throated swifts. Nearby is the Harmony Borax Works, where borax was king in the late 1800s. Wagons pulled by 20-mule teams hauled out tons of the grainy white substance, which was made into soap. Route 190 eventually crosses the floor of Death Valley and makes its way west, up the steep sides of the Panamint Range. There Wildrose Road follows Emigrant Canyon south to the trailhead to **Telescope Peak,** the highest point in the park. From the 11,049-foot summit, accessible on a seven-mile trail, hikers can see all of Death Valley and its bleached geologic bones.

The road south from the Wildrose Ranger Station becomes Route 178 again toward China Lake as it follows the western edge of a dry, barren lake bed, Searles Lake, created during the last Ice Age. Just south of the lake bed is **Trona Pinnacles National Natural Landmark❖,** which features some of the most spectacular tufa formations on the continent. A number of these calcium carbonate deposits that formed around the vents of hot springs 25,000 years ago are 100 feet tall and bizarrely shaped. Not surprisingly, the site has been a popular setting for science-fiction films.

WEST MOJAVE
Continuing on Route 178 to the intersection of Route 14, turn south for 27 miles to **Red Rock Canyon State Park❖,** site of some of the

---

RIGHT: *Far from lifeless, the sweeping sand dunes in Death Valley support dozens of species of plants, including grasses, shrubs, cacti, flowering perennials, and even trees, such as these tenacious mesquites.*

Mojave's most colorful geologic formations. The spectacularly eroded buttes and cliffs in this 25,000-acre park—the exposed sedimentary layers shading from eggshell white to flaming red to chocolate brown—have been used as backdrop for a number of motion pictures. Visitors can explore a gorge, a natural amphitheater, and numerous canyons that feature caprock ridges and fluted columns. Plant life here is typical of the western Mojave—creosote-bush scrub dotted with Joshua trees—and when rains are heavy, spring wildflowers bloom in mad profusion. Among the more unusual bird species spotted here are horned larks, Le Conte's thrashers, and canyon wrens. Adjacent to the park is the **Butterbredt Spring Wildlife Sanctuary❖,** a desert watering hole that attracts and protects a large number of birds.

South of Red Rock Canyon, 5 miles northeast of California City, is the **Desert Tortoise Research Natural Area❖,** a 39-square-mile preserve created specifically to protect this living symbol of the desert. Although the desert tortoise has called the Mojave home for the past two million years, habitat loss, livestock grazing, and off-road-vehicle use have put California's state reptile on the endangered species list. At one time, this site supported the highest known density of desert tortoises anywhere.

ABOVE: *Ancient images carved into the rocks by an early race of desert-dwelling hunters and gatherers are nearly hidden among the colorful lichen-draped boulders of Little Petroglyph Canyon near China Lake.*

Besides the desert tortoise, four distinct plant communities support 27 other species of reptiles, 23 mammals, 29 breeding birds in addition to many migrants, and more than 160 species of flowering plants. The state-listed rare Mojave ground squirrel depends on the preserve for survival, as does the golden eagle, desert kit fox, and the burrowing owl.

The shrub-covered flats and low, rolling hills of the preserve are dissected by dry washes and wash stringers that sometimes carry flash floods during the rainy season, usually from November to February. Elevations range from 1,920 to 3,100 feet. The western Mojave freezes about 80 days a year, and winter temperatures range from 15 to 57 degrees. In the summer, they can fluctuate 50 degrees to a high of 110. Average annual precipitation is two to five inches, and winds can howl in excess of 70 miles per hour.

The best time to visit is spring, when temperatures are most agreeable and desert tortoises are visible outside their burrows in the morning and late afternoon (from mid-June through February, they are usually deep in their burrows and seldom seen). The interpretative center contains illustrated displays explaining the site's natural history and is the trailhead for a series of connecting nature loops. Along the Main

47

Loop Trail through a creosote-bush scrub community, desert tortoises dig their burrows and scrape their resting pallets in front of the openings at the base of the creosote bushes. Abandoned burrows house other reptiles, including zebratailed, leopard, and side-blotched lizards and racer, gopher, glossy, common king, and longnosed snakes. Watch out for poisonous Mojave rattlesnakes and desert sidewinders (the latter leave a telltale S pattern in the sand).

Also coming to life in the spring are 15 different species of small perennial shrubs in the creosote-bush understory, including burrobush, goldenhead, cheese bush, winter fat, spiny hopsage, and Anderson thornbush, which has red berries. The desert floor is speckled by showy three-foot-high Mojave aster and desert candle. Saltbush scrub—allscale, scalebroom, Thurber sandpaper bush, shadscale, Mojave saltbush—grows in the washes and lower fans on the preserve's northern boundaries.

The vegetation supports a populous community of rodents such as large antelope and Mojave ground squirrels and smaller Merriam's kangaroo rats and long-tailed pocket, little pocket, and grasshopper mice. Plenty of birds inhabit the preserve too. Le Conte's thrashers, ash-throated flycatchers, Say's phoebes, horned larks, cactus wrens, and loggerhead shrikes live in the bushes, while turkey vultures, red-tailed hawks, and golden eagles soar overhead and roadrunners, Gambel's quail, and chukars stick to the ground.

After returning to Route 14, continue south and turn west on Lancaster Avenue to reach the **Antelope Valley California Poppy Reserve❖**. Tucked between the Tehachapi Mountains to the north and the San Gabriels to the south, this corner of high Mojave desert boasts one of the most opulent wildflower displays anywhere. Each spring, after plentiful winter rains, a thick mat of poppies, coreopsis, and goldfields turns the valley floor golden. Nearly 1,800 acres have been set aside here to preserve the official state flower. From March through early May, a charming interpretative center, designed to blend into the reserve's rounded hills, features breathtaking color photos and an informative videotape that tells the story of the area's floral treasures. Starting at the center, seven miles of trails loop through the spectacular rolling fields of orange, yellow, and gold flowers.

From the city of Lancaster, County Road N5 leads east to **Sad-**

48

ABOVE: *Slow and methodical, the desert tortoise is a creature of anti-quity that has lived in the desert for three million years; it is now threatened with extinction due to the destruction of its habitat.*

dleback Butte State Park❖, a 2,955-acre preserve that takes its name from a jagged 3,651-foot mound of granite. Here, ranger-led tours explore a healthy Joshua tree woodland, and each spring the desert floor is covered with fiddleneck, flowering beavertail cactus, desert dandelion, desert aster, and sand verbena. Although the pronghorn that used to graze here have disappeared, slow-moving desert tortoises can be found munching on desert flowers outside the entrances to their burrows. The most surprising thing about Saddleback Butte is that it's just an hour from downtown Los Angeles, a poignant reminder that southern California is, indeed, a desert at heart.

OVERLEAF: *For a few fleeting weeks each spring, orange California poppies and yellow wildflowers brighter than an Oriental carpet paint the Mojave Desert's Antelope Valley in a mad profusion of color.*

CALIFORNIA'S
SIERRA NEVADA

ven the most exaggerated superlatives fail to convey the size
and power of the longest and highest wall of granite on the
planet, the Sierra Nevada. What words can adequately por-
tray the sheer majesty of this 430-mile-long curtain of stone?
What verbs can accurately import the actions of millennia of fire and ice
that shaped these rocks into jagged spires, polished domes, and cathe-
dral-like ridgelines? And what adjectives can measure the Sierra's lofty
heights—the 11 peaks that soar more than 14,000 feet, the 500 that
tower more than 2 miles high? Even the Sierra Nevada's most celebrated
author declined to match wits with the mountains' geologic grandeur,
confining himself instead to the poetry of its aesthetic qualities. In *My
First Summer in the Sierras*, John Muir's description of his first trip to
Yosemite some 125 years ago still rings true today:

> And from the eastern boundary of this vast golden flower bed rose
> the mighty Sierra, miles in height, and so gloriously colored and so
> radiant, it seemed not clothed with light, but wholly composed of it,
> like the wall of some celestial city. Along the top and extending a
> good way down, was a rich pearl-gray belt of snow; below it a belt
> of blue and dark purple, marking the extension of the forests; and
> stretching along the base of the range a broad belt of rose-purple;

LEFT: *With its sheer granite face rising majestically over the clear
Merced River below, El Capitan is one of Yosemite National Park's
most imposing landmarks and a magnet for rock climbers worldwide.*

all these colors, from the blue sky to the yellow valley smoothly blending as they do in a rainbow, making a wall of light ineffably fine. Then it seemed to me that the Sierra should be called, not the Nevada or Snowy Range, but the Range of Light. And after ten years of wandering and wondering in the heart of it, rejoicing in its glorious floods of light, the white beams of the morning streaming through the passes, the noonday radiance on the crystal rocks, the flush of the alpenglow, and the irised spray of countless waterfalls, it still seems above all others the Range of Light.

No wonder the Sierra Nevada has been beckoning natural-history lovers since the days of John Muir. Few other mountain ranges can compare. The Sierra is so big that it easily encompasses 8 national forests, 3 national parks, 14 wilderness areas, and more than a dozen state parks, monuments, and recreation areas. In this chapter, the route encompasses the Sierra's crown jewels, including Yosemite, Sequoia, and Kings Canyon national parks as well as other wondrous sites.

Not only does the Sierra form the geologic backbone of California, but it provides the state's lifeblood as well. Snowmelt from 66 glaciers and snowpacks averaging 37 feet deep each winter launches dozens of rivers and hundreds of streams that supply the state's cities and farmlands. No greater natural irrigation system exists. In the Sierra, water plunges over 4 of the world's 10 highest waterfalls and cascades down 16 major rivers—some of the most turbulent ever found, as the legions of white-water kayakers and rafters that challenge them each spring can testify.

The Sierra Nevada also provides a home for an amazing array of wildlife species because a number of vegetation zones—upper Sonoran, Transition, Canadian, Hudsonian, and Arctic Alpine—exist in these mountains. Traveling over a pass in the Sierra is akin to driving from Mexico to the Arctic Circle. In just a few miles, vegetation changes from chaparral, currant, and digger pine to oak, willow, cottonwood, and ponderosa pine to Douglas and red fir, lodgepole pine, and incense cedar to heather to phlox. Each zone supports a distinct

OVERLEAF: *High in the Sierra Nevada range, melting snow and ice create mirror-surfaced alpine lakes in the sawtoothed Great Western Divide, a jagged stretch of 13,000-foot peaks in Sequoia National Park.*

THE SIERRA
NEVADA

25   0   25 Miles

25   0   25 Kilometers

community of animals. Quail, coyotes, and jackrabbits live in the lower elevations, mountain lions, black bears, and ringtails in the middle reaches, and pikas, Sierra bighorn sheep, and marmots above tree line.

The formation of the Sierra Nevada is one of geology's most dramatic stories. Some 500 million years ago, sediment was deposited in layers on the ocean floor at the western edge of the future North American continent. About 200 million years ago, this submerged sedimentary layer was forced under the continental land mass—an act called subduction by plate tectonic theorists—causing it to become very hot and liquefy. Over time the molten mass shot up under the edge of the continent and formed a chain of ancestral volcanoes, cooling and hardening into granite covered by sedimentary rock. The magma that fed these volcanoes was a small portion of a huge series of plutons (molten bodies well beneath the earth's surface) that slowly cooled and crystallized into the Sierran granite. For the next 55 million years, wind and rain eroded the sediments and left the underlying granite exposed. Then, about 25 million years ago, the land along today's San Andreas fault began to move, pushing the mountain range rapidly skyward and tilting it westward. When the earth grew colder 2 to 3 million years ago, glaciers sculpted and scoured the range to its present configuration: a land of silvery peaks, glacially gouged U-shaped canyons, and exfoliated spires, domes, and cliffs.

The Sierra Nevada occupies a good chunk of California, stretching roughly from Bakersfield in the south to the Middle Fork of the Feather River in the north. And even that point really isn't the final terminus of the Sierra because geologists believe that powerful forces cleaved the range in two about 140 million years ago. A distance of some 60 miles now separates the rocks found in the Sierra Nevada from identical ones in the Klamath Range to the northwest. From a high-flying bird's perspective, the range is shaped like a mountain lion's powerful foreleg, the paw pointed toward the Pacific.

So rugged is the Sierra, so inaccessible at times, that exploring it by automobile requires dividing the range into three digestible sections: the

RIGHT: *Visitors crane their necks in Sequoia National Park to admire one of the world's largest living things, the 275-foot-tall General Sherman tree, a giant sequoia that sprouted some 2,300 years ago.*

southern Sierra, the Lake Tahoe area, and the Backside, as residents call its eastern slope. This itinerary heads north from Bakersfield, tracking the southern Sierra as it begins in desert and elevates quickly into Sequoia and Kings Canyon national parks, where lush forests are filled with giant sequoias and equally giant mountain peaks. Continuing north, the route visits the majestic waterfalls of Yosemite National Park and explores the thick forests on the southern shores of Lake Tahoe, one of the world's largest mountain lakes. Finally, it returns south along the Backside—a land of snowcapped escarpments whose near-vertical walls rise impossibly from the Great Basin Desert floor—stopping at Mono Lake, a forest of ancient bristlecone pines, and the Kern River Preserve. Although John Muir called it the Range of Light, the Sierra Nevada is equally deserving of the sobriquet Range of Ranges.

SEQUOIA AND KINGS CANYON NATIONAL PARKS

From the oil-refining and agricultural city of Bakersfield, Route 65 runs straight through the San Joaquin Valley and along the foothills of the southern Sierra Nevada—also called the Greenhorn Mountains—to Route 198 east into **Sequoia National Park❖**, the first of three in the Sierra. In its 402,108 acres, the park contains the world's largest tree and the tallest mountain in the 48 contiguous states. Created in 1890 to protect both of these giants, Sequoia is the second-oldest national park after Yellowstone.

The park's namesake, of course, is what draws most of the two million annual visitors. The giant sequoia is a survivor of the last Ice Age, scion of an ancient lineage of huge trees that mantled much of the globe millions of years ago when dinosaurs roamed the earth. Today, it grows naturally in only 75 groves between 5,000 and 7,000 feet on the west slope of the Sierra Nevada. In volume of total wood, the giant sequoia stands alone as the largest living thing on the planet. Although at least two other tree species live longer, one has a greater diameter, and three grow taller, none is larger.

Giant sequoias are not the only attraction in the park. From Route 198 at Hammond, Mineral King Road winds steeply up along the east fork of the Kaweah River for 25 miles to the **Mineral King** section of the park, which was added in 1978 after concerned citizens blocked a bid to develop it as a ski resort. The area gets its name from the optimistic miners who flocked here in the 1870s, lured by the promise of

ABOVE: *A meandering Mosquito Creek drains the Mosquito Lakes Basin in the Mineral King section of Sequoia National Park. The ruggedly scenic area was annexed in 1978 to block development of a ski resort.*

another Comstock Lode. Although Mineral King never produced much silver, the scenery is some of the richest in the Sierra. The twisting 100-year-old road reaches the very edge of the high country, a land of subalpine meadows, towering timberline peaks, and dazzling lakes. To experience the real magic of the High Sierra, leave the car at the end of the road and take to the trails. Those leading to Sawtooth Pass, Crystal Lake, Eagle Lake, and Timber Gap climb steeply from the valley floor, but the views at the top are worth the effort.

Route 198 enters the main part of the park at Ash Mountain. Renamed the Generals Highway, this nature loop connects Sequoia with its northern neighbor, Kings Canyon National Park, except in winter. **Generals Highway** through Sequoia National Park leads to a grove containing four of the world's five largest trees, aptly named **Giant Forest** by John Muir. On his first exploration, he wrote: "When I entered this sublime wilderness the day was nearly done, the trees with rosy, glowing countenances seemed to be hushed and thoughtful,

61

as if waiting in conscious religious dependence on the sun, and one naturally walked softly and awe-stricken among them." The largest of the four is the General Sherman, which is estimated to be up to 2,300 years old. This club-shaped ancient has a maximum basal diameter of 36 feet and a height of 275 feet; its largest limb is almost 7 feet around. When botanists get out their calculators, they find that the tree has a total trunk volume of more than 50,000 cubic feet and a total weight of 2.7 million pounds! Each year the General Sherman adds enough wood growth to make a 60-foot tree of the usual proportions.

ABOVE: *A favorite of John Muir, the American dipper dives fearlessly into waterfalls and walks under rushing mountain streams to feed on insect larvae and small fish.*

RIGHT: *Jagged as an emperor's crown, Mount Whitney rises in the Sierra crest, looming above a trail camp.*

Plan to spend at least a couple of days at Giant Forest. On any one of the myriad trails winding through this section, keep an eye out for mule deer browsing in sun-dappled meadows; listen for the agitated chirp of the chickaree, a tree squirrel that makes its home in the giant sequoias and feasts on the cones (a giant sequoia can produce 40,000 of them); and scan the sky for Steller's jays and western tanagers. A favorite hike climbs Moro Rock Trail, 300 vertical feet to the top of a dome-shaped granite monolith that rises 4,000 feet above the valley floor and offers a stunning view of the surrounding mountains and countryside.

The more adventurous can continue to the High Sierra Trail, which climbs quickly above tree line from Crescent Meadow to a series of alpine lakes surrounded by 13,000-plus-foot peaks that mark the saw-toothed Great Western Divide. The most formidable-looking of these is Black Kaweah. The trail continues to **Mount Whitney**—at 14,494 feet, the tallest in the continental United States. A moderately difficult 10-mile trail leads to its summit from base camp. Five other 14,000-footers flank it on either side. Together, they are guaranteed to awe, inspire, and humble any who gaze upon them.

The Generals Highway winds north through the western corner of the park and crosses into a detached section of adjacent **Kings Canyon National Park❖**. This isolated square of the 459,995-acre park is called **Grant Grove** for its most famous resident, the General Grant giant sequoia, also known as the Nation's Christmas Tree. The grove was protected as General Grant National Park in 1890, after loggers felled many of the colossal trees. Today visitors can see the Centennial Stump—all that is left of a giant sequoia cut in 1875 for the Philadelphia centennial celebration of the American Revolution—and the basin where enormous stumps stand like tombstones. Merged into newly created Kings Canyon National Park in 1940, Grant Grove features a visitor center and a number of short nature trails. Those who can spend the day should take the 10-mile loop to Redwood Canyon, which leads to one of the finest and least visited groves of sequoias in the Sierra.

A 30-mile dead-end road, Route 180, follows a steeply rugged river canyon from Grant Grove to Cedar Grove. The South Fork of the Kings River—which Spanish missionaries named *El Rio de los Santos Reyes* (the River of the Holy Kings)—furrows the park in rock-lined, water-filled glory. From the canyon's edge, the river below looks like a white ribbon furling and fluttering. In the steepest part of the canyon—the depth ranges from 4,000 to 8,000 feet—the South Fork drops several times faster than the Colorado River as it passes through the Grand Canyon.

The highway crosses the South Fork and runs along the south shore at the entrance to Cedar Grove, which contains four campgrounds, a village, and a lodge and is the center of summer activity in the park. Horseback riding is offered for visiting explorers, and a one-way auto nature trail runs east to west along the north side of the river starting just past Roaring River Falls, where the Kings Canyon Highway crosses the South Fork for the last time.

The River Trail leads to **Zumwalt Meadow,** a nearly flat six-mile-long valley whose sylvan setting poses a stark contrast to the rocky walls of the steep river canyon and the treeless granitic peaks that soar

---

LEFT: *Wild lupines bloom bright and purple in a carpet of cones and needles shed by ponderosa pines at Kings Canyon National Park.*

OVERLEAF: *A visitor's first view of Yosemite Valley encompasses the park's major landmarks: El Capitan, Half Dome, and Bridalveil Fall.*

ABOVE: *Theodore Roosevelt accompanied nature writer John Muir to Yosemite in 1903 on a trip that inspired the president to increase federal protection for Yosemite Valley.*

RIGHT: *Glaciers cut Yosemite Valley deeper than the surrounding terrain, creating such spectacular cascades as Vernal Fall.*

behind it. Another favorite day hike, a bit more strenuous, is the trail to **Mist Falls,** which penetrates the mixed conifer forest that cloaks the park at mid-elevation. The forest contains at least ten different species of evergreen trees, from the ponderosa pine and incense cedar that predominate in the lowest portions to white fir, sugar pine, and Jeffrey pine in the better-watered locations at the same elevations that support the giant sequoia, to red fir above 7,000 feet. Above 8,000 feet, western white pine replaces sugar pine.

Wildlife abounds in the mixed conifer forest, where trees house great horned owls, pileated woodpeckers, yellow-bellied sapsuckers, and red-breasted nuthatches. Black bears, bobcats, mule deer, bighorn sheep, yellow-bellied marmots, Clark's nutcrackers, and mountain yellow-legged frogs appear along the trails leading out of the canyon to the remote, isolated northern corner of the park. At the very tip is seldom-visited **Evolution Basin.** The four towering peaks ringing this depression are named Mount Darwin, Mount Wallace, Mount Huxley, and Mount Spencer in honor of the famous evolutionists.

YOSEMITE NATIONAL PARK

The third Sierra Nevada national park, one of the nation's oldest and most famous, lies north of Kings Canyon via Routes 180 west to Fresno and 41 north. **Yosemite National Park❖** was established on October 1, 1890, thanks largely to the efforts of John Muir and eastern

magazine editor Robert Underwood Johnson, who publicized the need to protect this unique place. Although he was Yosemite's most vocal admirer, Muir wasn't the first immigrant to see it. A party of explorers led by Joseph Reddeford Walker looked down on Yosemite Valley from its north rim in 1833, but not until 1851 did the first non-native settlers reach the valley floor. Previously, Yosemite's principal human residents were Miwok Indians, and anthropologists estimate that Native Americans had resided in the Yosemite region for 4,000 years. The Miwok were hunter-gatherers who established permanent villages along the Merced River. ("Yosemite" may be a corruption of the Miwok word for grizzly bear—*uzumati*—or a version of the Ahwahneechee word *Yo-che-ma-te,* which means "some among them are killers" of bears.)

Lured by tales of towering trees, sheer granite cliffs, tinsel-like waterfalls, and lush meadows, Yosemite's first tourists arrived in 1855 and were not disappointed. Today, 94 percent of Yosemite's 748,542 acres is designated wilderness. The park protects 1,400 species of flowering plants, 37 species of trees, 242 birds, 74 mammals, 10 fish,

CLOCKWISE FROM TOP: *The Sierra abounds with wildflowers: evening primroses in summer meadows, Kelly's tiger lilies in the mountains, and columbines in the woods.* LEFT: *Harlequin and blue lupines colonize a fire-blackened pine grove in Yosemite National Park.*

and 24 amphibians and reptiles. There are 318 lakes and 880 miles of rivers and streams.

From the south, start at **Mariposa Grove,** the largest of three giant sequoia stands in Yosemite. Park at the grove and ride the open-air trams, which operate approximately May through October, to see the 300-ton Grizzly Giant presiding over the stand of 500 cinnamon-barked beauties. Estimated to be 2,700 years old, it stretches 209 feet into the sky with a trunk bulging to more than 28 feet in diameter. The Mariposa Grove Museum offers insights and information on the region's natural history.

Just north is Wawona (the Miwok word for "big tree" and the phonetic spelling of the tribe's call to the owls, which Miwok believed to be guardian spirits of the giant sequoia). Settled very early in the park's history, the historic community of Wawona became an important stopover on the stagecoach route. The rambling Wawona Hotel, built in 1879, is the oldest resort hotel operating in California. Also in the area are cabins and cottages for rent, as well as a campground. From Wawona, which occupies a beautiful meadow nestled near the South

Fork of the Merced River, the Chilnualna Trail leads four miles uphill through the woods to **Chilnualna Falls,** a several-hundred-foot-high cascade. Belted kingfishers and American dippers ply the waterways for meals. Favorites of John Muir's, dippers, also called water ouzels, are fun to watch. Named for their habit of constantly bobbing up and down, these robin-sized birds fly into a stream and walk upstream underwater along the bottom searching for food.

Here the forest is filled with ponderosa pine, incense cedar, and Jeffrey pine, which can be distinguished from the ponderosa by its vanilla fragrance. The pineapple-sized cones that fall from the sugar pines can reach a foot in length and weigh as much as four pounds. Native Americans ate the cone's sugary resin and also made glue from it.

North of Wawona is Glacier Point Road (open only in summer), a 16-mile drive that leads to the top of the sheer southern wall of Yosemite Valley. Here visitors can see the valley floor 3,200 feet below and breathtaking vistas in all directions (no better view of the park is accessible by automobile). Exhibits explain the geologic processes that shaped Yosemite, and signposts identify all the major peaks. The tallest is 13,114-foot Mount Lyell.

Encompassing seven square miles and scenic beauty galore, **Yosemite Valley** is the center of activity for the park. In the summer months, it also contains plenty of people. Four million flock to the park each year. Consequently, visitors are advised to park their cars at Curry Village and travel to the most popular sites on free shuttle buses.

The logical starting point is the Valley Visitor Center, where visitors can obtain information and see the Yosemite Museum Gallery, the Indian Cultural Exhibit, and the Indian Village behind the center. **Lower Yosemite Falls** is an easy quarter-mile walk from the shuttle pullout. Together with its upper section, Yosemite Falls measures 2,425 feet, the fifth-highest waterfall in the world. The valley is awash in cascading water. Even more remarkable is the number of free-leaping falls—those whose descent is not broken on intervening ledges or outcroppings. Yosemite's geology is responsible for its hydrologic abundance. Although glaciers carved the park's major watercourses such as Yosemite Valley very deeply, lateral tributary streams cut much more slowly, creating "hanging valleys." Streams and creeks that originally fed directly into primary rivers were left on high ground

ABOVE: *In fall, the leaves of black oaks that cluster in the woods and meadows of Yosemite Valley mimic the colors of New England, turning gold and crimson as cool temperatures return to the High Sierra.*

and forced to spill over the brinks of lofty cliffs to reach the rivers in the deep canyons below.

Happy Isles Nature Center is the trailhead for day hikes to Vernal Fall, Nevada Fall, and **Half Dome,** surely the most readily identifiable feature in the park and a textbook example of "sheeting" and exfoliation. Sheeting, a type of "jointing," or rock fracture, is responsible for much of Yosemite's striking scenery. Sheeting describes the cracking of a rock along curved surfaces parallel to the surface of the rock, whereas jointing usually occurs up and down as well as in two horizontal directions. Unlike the sharp, ragged peaks of jointed rock seen on Mount Whitney, Half Dome was formed when layers of granite exfoliated, or leafed away like layers of onion. Exfoliation is the result of

73

ABOVE: *Some 5,000 mountain lions now roam California's wilderness areas. Human encounters with the sleek, seldom-seen predator are increasing as civilization encroaches on the cat's natural habitat.*

pressure release as outlying rocks are stripped away. The granite, originally formed miles beneath the surface under tremendous pressure, expands like a spring when the rock above it is removed. One of the best views of Half Dome is from **Mirror Lake,** a mile-long walk from the shuttle stop. There is also a one-to-two-hour hike around the lake.

After leaving Yosemite Valley, continue north on Route 41 and head east on Tioga Pass Road (Route 120), the most southerly east-west crossing in the Sierra. Built in 1883 by the Great Consolidated Silver Company, this former wagon road splits Yosemite National Park in two. Because it reaches an elevation of 9,945 feet at Tioga Pass, it is open only a few months each year. Lined with campgrounds, trailheads, lakes, streams, and meadows, Tioga Pass Road offers some of the most stunning views in the park. At 8,600 feet lies **Tuolumne Meadows,** a 2.5-mile-long subalpine basin ringed by granite domes that is the heart of Yosemite's high country. The crystal-clear Tuolumne River, the source of San Francisco's drinking water, flows through the meadow, and hikers make the area a base camp for their assaults on Yosemite's backcountry.

LAKE TAHOE AREA

To leave Yosemite, retrace the spectacular scenery of Tioga Pass Road to the park's western boundary; head west on Route 120 and then

74

ABOVE: *Although classified in the order Carnivora, the black bear— which also comes in shades of brown and cinnamon—mainly forages for grubs, roots, and berries in heavily forested parts of the Sierra.*

north on Route 49, California's appropriately named Golden Highway. This winding two-lane blacktop parallels the crest of the Sierra around the 1,800-foot level and links dozens of historic mining towns that sprang to life with the discovery of gold at Sutter's Mill in 1848. Columbia, Angels Camp, Coloma, and Nevada City—towns made famous by the writings of Mark Twain—offer a revealing glimpse into California's exciting human past, as well as the powerful geologic forces that created the lustrous metal that precipitated one of the greatest human migrations of all times.

The Sierra Nevada foothills are awash in gold by the grace of granite. The preparation for gold ore to form occurred about 150 million years ago, when the still-evolving mountains fractured. Mineralizing solutions rose from the depths and traveled along cracks and breaks opened by these fractures. When the granite magma cooled, it left behind veins of gold-bearing quartz and other metamorphic rock—the Mother Lode, as miners called it. In many places, the heavier-than-rock gold nuggets collected in river gravel as streams eroded the mountainsides, making them easy pickings for the prospectors. By the turn of the century, California's gold fields had produced the modern-day equivalent of $25 billion in gold.

Along one of the Sierra Nevada rivers lies a treasure of another kind—giant sequoias. **Calaveras Big Trees State Park❖,** off Route 4 northeast from Angels Camp along the North Fork of the Stanislaus River protects hundreds of these stately colossi in two adjacent groves. The

trees were discovered by European settlers in 1853 when a hunter named A. T. Dowd chased a wounded grizzly into what is now the North Grove of the park. Stunned by the sight of trees 100 feet in circumference, Dowd stopped chasing the bear and spent the remainder of the day exploring the surrounding forest, later returning to the mining towns in the Sierra foothills to tell whoever would listen about his amazing discovery. In no time, others flocked to the grove. Newspapers and magazines in America and Europe carried stories about the newfound giants, often exaggerating the already astonishing facts. Unfortunately, exploiting rather than protecting the trees was the order of the day, and much to his disgust, Dowd saw his "discovery tree" cut down and pieces of it shipped east for exhibition. Someone built a bowling alley atop its stump, as well as a covered pavilion where dances were held.

ABOVE: *Found mainly in the West, the brazen Steller's jay sports a long black crest and dark blue feathers.*

RIGHT: *A towering white fir tree shades the shoreline of Fallen Leaf Lake in the Desolation Wilderness Area southwest of Lake Tahoe.*

Well into the 1870s, the **North Grove** remained the most famous and popular group of giant sequoias, and eventually, the 150 trees were protected by the state. An even larger stand of trees, the **South Grove,** was classified as a "natural preserve" by the State Park Commission in 1984, the highest level of protection afforded to land within the park system. An easy one-mile self-guided nature trail wanders through the North Grove, and the self-guided South Grove Trail begins a mile from the end of the paved road at Beaver Creek. Of the other interesting trails that wind through the 6,000-acre park, the Lava Bluffs Trail passes bold outcrops of lava that rise above the surrounding pine forest, remnants of the massive lava flows occurring here several million years ago when the

main fault block that forms the Sierra Nevada range tilted up to its present position.

After hopscotching north over river canyons that drain the western slope of the Sierra, Route 49 intersects Route 50, the principal road between Sacramento and south Lake Tahoe. East on Route 50 at the 3,500-foot level in a foothill transition zone lies **Jenkinson Lake❖** and the **Sly Park Recreation Area❖.** The 640-acre lake—actually a reservoir that supplies water for El Dorado County—is surrounded by a dense understory of manzanita, mountain misery, dogwood, toyon, and willow. Composing the forest covering are stands of yellow pine, white fir, incense cedar, Douglas fir madrona, valley oak, and California black oak. The lake and its surrounding plant communities provide habitat for a wide assortment of wildlife, and a trail skirting the lake's eight-mile shoreline features scenic stops for viewing bald eagles, ospreys, and sharp-shinned hawks. Stocked with rainbow, brown, and Mackinaw trout, the lake attracts plenty of waterfowl and shorebirds, including spotted sandpipers, common goldeneyes, grebes, and buffleheads. Mourning doves, quail, and wild turkeys scurry through the dense thickets of manzanita and mountain misery while black-tailed deer seek cover there. California gray squirrels and striped skunks dwell in the forested areas, as do dozens of bird species, among them pileated woodpeckers, wrentits, Nashville warblers, and black-headed grosbeaks.

For thousands of years the abundant acorns, fish, and game attracted Maidu and Miwok Indians, who used holes in the rocks to grind their acorns into an edible paste. In 1848, early Mormon pioneer James Calvin Sly passed through on his way to Salt Lake City. His route, called the Mormon Emigrant Trail, proved to be the best way to go east from California. Livestock grazed in the meadow in the nineteenth century, and the dam, which created the lake, was completed in 1955.

Farther east on Route 50 toward 7,377-foot Echo Summit, the Sierra's trademark granitic peaks become visible once again. Just north of the highway sprawls the 64,000-acre **Desolation Wilderness❖,** which lives up to its name. Because few trees grow here, shade is provided by a jumble of huge boulders gleaming white in the high-altitude sun. Joined by three other towering summits, Pyramid Peak rises 9,983 feet along the wilderness area's southern boundary. The region is laced by countless streams flowing in and out of approximately 130 alpine lakes, some as large as 900 acres. So stark, so beautifu is this wilderness area, yet so accessible by road, that it has become one of the most popular destinations for backpackers in the whole Sierra. Consequently, the Forest Service has had to limit overnight visitors between June 15 and September 8. Only 700 permits are granted, half issued up to 90 days in advance, half on the date.

Nestled below and slightly east of these granite peaks is **Lake Tahoe❖,** which takes its name from the Washoe Indian word for "big water." At 6,229 feet it is the second-highest lake of its size in the world, and so deep that if the World Trade Center towers stood on the bottom, their roofs would still be underwater. The great depth creates crystalline waters and keeps the lake from freezing. The setting is so beautiful that the shores of Lake Tahoe have undergone tremendous development over the years—19 ski resorts now cling to the surrounding mountainsides, while high-rise casinos and hotels line the southern shoreline.

Remnants of Tahoe's natural identity hold fast on the west side of the lake, however, where just off Route 89 are the **Emerald Bay** and **D. L. Bliss❖** state parks. Occupying six miles of lake frontage at often photographed Emerald Bay and totaling 1,830 acres, the pair are linked by trails that wind through spectacular alpine scenery. The Rubicon Trail follows the rugged shoreline, skirting enormous rock outcroppings that rise from water's edge. Pied-billed grebes, mergansers, mallard, and other migratory waterfowl feed in the protected coves; Canada geese nest on Fannette Island, just offshore; and bald eagles visit in winter. One of the Emerald Bay's main attractions is a 38-room Norse mansion, Vikingsholm. Made of hand-hewn wood with a sod roof, this incongruous sight is the finest example of the medieval Scandinavian architectural style in the United States.

The Eagle Falls Trail, which climbs to 7,400 feet and an impressive cascade that drops several hundred feet, leads through a healthy forest of Jeffrey, sugar, and lodgepole pine, red and white fir, incense cedar, black cottonwood, and aspen. Juncos, western tanagers, mountain chickadees, and white-headed woodpeckers live in these woods as do chipmunks, golden-mantled ground squirrels, beavers, and coyotes. Pine marten (thick-furred cousins of skunks, badgers, and mink) prey on white-footed mice.

Return southeast on Route 89 over 7,740-foot Luther Pass to the town of Markleeville and **Grover Hot Springs State Park❖**. The 560-acre park occupies Hot Springs Valley, a lovely alpine meadow surrounded by the **Toiyabe National Forest** and ringed on three sides by volcanic peaks, including 10,023-foot Hawkins Peak to the northwest and 9,417-foot Markleeville Peak. Since the 1850s visitors have made pilgrimages here to soak in a soothing pool fed by six mineral springs resulting from the faulting that occurred when the Sierra Nevada began to rise. Surface water courses through the cracks in the earth's crust until it reaches hot rock thousands of feet below; then it bubbles back to the surface, dissolving minerals along its way. At the park, the water—which contains sodium, sulfate, calcium, iron, and alumina—is diverted into a concrete pool and regulated to about 102 degrees Fahrenheit. Devotees credit it with a long list of curative powers.

A number of trails crisscross the valley, and a self-guided loop describing the area's natural history begins at the campground bridge. Flowering plants in the meadow grassland include asters and lilies, bordered along the edges by Jeffrey pines and white firs. Among the resident mammals are coyotes, black bears, bobcats, and long-tailed weasels. In winter, the meadow and adjacent hot springs attract cross-country skiers.

THE BACKSIDE: THE EASTERN SIERRA

Continuing south, Route 89 crosses the crest of the Sierra Nevada at 8,314-foot Monitor Pass, descending the steep escarpment on the eastern side to intersect Route 395. This scenic byway runs south along what locals call the Backside of the Sierra. Granite-faced walls soar skyward west of the highway while the Great Basin Desert spreads to the east. Farther south, just past Conway Summit, an ancient inland sea sparkles invitingly.

Covering approximately 60 square miles, **Mono Lake❖** appears barren at first. Delicate calcium-carbonate knobs and spires of tufa (porous rock) dot the lake and shoreline. A black volcanic island rises from the water, and a patch of lifeless craters extends to the south. But closer inspection reveals abundant wildlife in the form of insects, brine shrimp, and birds. Because Mono Lake has no outlet, its water is salty and alkaline—2.5 times saltier and 100 times more alkaline than seawater. Over the 700,000 years since the lake was formed (it is among the oldest lakes in North America), a unique brine fly and several species of brine shrimp have evolved, providing food for numerous

ABOVE: *Created 100,000 years ago by cracking, cooling lava, the unusual basaltic columns at Devils Postpile National Monument have from three to seven sides and sometimes reach as high as 60 feet.*

bird species, including eared grebes and phalaropes. Snowy plover nest on the east shore while 50,000 California gulls visit Negit Island and nearby islets, the largest gull rookery in the state. The brine fly also supported Native Americans. In fact, the Yokut, who lived west of the Sierra crest, gave to the local Paiute people the word *mono,* which means "fly-pupae eaters."

Mono Lake's tufa towers, eerie spires that seem to belong to another world, were formed when calcium-rich water from submerged springs mixed with carbonates in the salty lake water and are now exposed because the water level has dropped. Surface evaporation totals four feet per year. In 1941, the City of Los Angeles began diverting water from four of the seven streams that empty into the lake, and since then, the lake has dropped more than 40 feet. Guided naturalist tours are given regularly at the **Mono Lake Tufa State Reserve❖** on the south shore. A few miles away, a short but steep trail leads to the top

OVERLEAF: *An approaching storm accentuates the dramatic look of the tufa spires at Mono Lake. This otherworldly landscape surrounds a salty inland sea on the high desert plateau east of the Sierra Nevada.*

of Panum Crater for a good view of the Mono craters. A boardwalk trail beginning at **Mono Lake County Park** leads through squirrel grass to a marsh and more tufa towers at the lake's eroded pumice beaches. Along the trail, watch for Belding's ground squirrels and coyotes.

A different side of vulcanism exists at **Devils Postpile National Monument❖,** 17 miles west of Route 395 on Route 203 near the resort community of Mammoth Lakes, where a bank of 60-foot-high vertical basalt columns stand like the pipes of a gigantic organ. The columns, which have from three to seven sides, were formed about 100,000 years ago when basalt lava erupted in the valley of the Middle Fork of the San Joaquin River. Lava flowing away from the vent filled the valley to a depth of 400 feet, and as the lava cooled and shrank, surface cracks formed. Each crack branched when it reached a critical length, forming a pattern with other cracks on the surface of the flow. After the surface cracks deepened and shaped the postlike columns, some 10,000 years ago a glacier traveled down the river valley and overrode the fractured mass of lava. The moving ice carved away one side of the postpile, exposing a sheer wall of columns.

In the 800-acre monument, rangers lead tours and hikers can walk to the summit of the postpile to see the tops of the columns, which have been polished by the passing glacier. The resulting natural floor looks as though it were paved with polygonal tiles. One would have to travel to Giant's Causeway in Northern Ireland or Fingal's Cave in Scotland to find a similar display of columnar-jointed basalt.

A trail from the postpile leads south along the Middle Fork of the San Joaquin to **Rainbow Falls,** where the river drops 101 feet over a cliff of andesite and rhyodacite (volcanic rocks). The falls were created after the last Ice Age, when the river cut channels in the lava down to granite about 1,500 feet west of its present course, leaving a cliff of rhyodacite on its eastern bank. Then, some distance upstream, the river was diverted from its bed to follow its present path until it returned to the old channel by cascading down the cliff it had earlier cut.

North of the postpile is a group of mineral springs lying on a gravel

---

RIGHT: *Sunset casts a golden glow over Mono Lake and its tufa formations, created when calcium in submerged springs mixed with carbonates in the salty water. The spires emerged when water levels fell.*

In the Schulman Grove of the Ancient Bristlecone Pine Forest in the White Mountains, one of the wizened trees sprouted nearly 4,700 years ago and ranks among the oldest living things on earth.

bar called **Soda Springs.** Gases driven upward from deep within the earth combine with groundwater to produce cold and highly carbonated mineralized springs. As it is exposed to air, iron in the water oxidizes and colors the reddish brown gravel.

Just north of the town of Bishop, Route 395 intersects Route 6, which leads north about five miles via Five Bridges Road to **Fish Slough❖.** Fed by three natural springs, this unique sanctuary harbors two species of endangered fish, the Owens pupfish and Owens tui chub. A lush oasis in the middle of an otherwise arid landscape known as the Volcanic Tableland, the slough was designated an Area of Critical Environmental Concern by the Bureau of Land Management in 1982 to protect not only the fish, but also several plant species that are candidates for protection under the federal Endangered Species Act. The Fish Slough milk vetch grows here and nowhere else in the world. Other unique species are the alkali mariposa lily, Mono buckwheat, alkali cordgrass, Hot Spring fimbristylis, Great Basin centaurium, King's ivesia, and silverleaf milk vetch.

At the water's edge, visitors can view the tiny fish that live in the crystal pools. When the Owens River ran freely, the Owens pupfish was found throughout the Owens Valley. Then, about 50 years ago, the City of Los Angeles purchased a corridor of land down the center of the valley and diverted the river into the 340-mile-long concrete-lined Los Angeles Aqueduct. The diversion of water doomed most of the region's wetlands and riparian habitat, and along with them, their resident wildlife. Indeed, the Owens pupfish was believed extinct by 1948 because the small population at Fish Slough wasn't discovered until 1964. Surviving in warm, shallow water by feeding on insect larvae and and other invertebrates, the two-inch pupfish can be recognized by their distinctive start-stop swimming style. Another survivor clinging to life here is the Owens tui chub, which is at least twice as big as the pupfish. Two other native fish species weren't so lucky. The Owens speckled dace and the Owens sucker, once found here, are now thought to be extinct.

The remaining marshy area provides a home for such other wildlife species as cinnamon teal, mallard, ruddy ducks, pintail, and gadwalls, which stop off during spring and fall migration. Great blue herons and American bitterns feed on aquatic life. The boulders and cliffs surrounding Fish Slough offer excellent perching and nesting sites for golden eagles, red-tailed hawks, and northern harriers.

Farther south on Route 395 and then east on Route 168 grow the oldest trees on earth, bristlecone pines. In the steep, wind-swept White Mountains is the 28,000-acre **Ancient Bristlecone Pine Forest❖.** Tree ring patterns suggest that the oldest of these twisted ancients are in the 4,700-year range, placing them among the oldest living things on the planet. The pines grow on the upper rocky slopes of the White Mountains, one of the least visited yet most beautiful ranges in the state. Elevations reach over 14,000 feet. The **Schulman Grove** is home to the 4,700-year-old Methuselah tree and contains a visitor center; the largest bristlecone lives in the **Patriarch Grove.**

The fierce winds sweeping this range twist the tree limbs into gnarled shapes resembling the arms of supplicants reaching toward the heavens. In late spring and summer, songbirds such as mountain chickadees, white-breasted nuthatches, hermit thrushes, mountain bluebirds, and violet-green swallows perch on them, and olive-sided flycatchers, western wood-pewees, and Pacific slope flycatchers swoop among them for insects. Common barn, western screech, and great horned owls are permanent residents, as are northern pygmy, burrow-

LEFT: *No bigger than a house cat, the San Joaquin kit fox faces extinction because agricultural and suburban development have plowed under and paved over its native habitat.*

ing, and long-eared owls, though they are much less common. Resident predators include sharp-shinned, Cooper's, and red-tailed hawks, as well as golden eagles, northern harriers, and prairie falcons.

About 110 miles south on Route 395, Route 178 leads west over Walker Pass to the Nature Conservancy's **Kern River Preserve❖,** just outside the tiny town of Weldon. This 1,127-acre area protects a unique riparian forest—the lush green woodlands that grow in river floodplains. Among the richest of all habitats, riparian forests are also becoming the rarest, casualties of a civilization that relentlessly commandeers more and more space for agriculture, industry, housing, highways, airports, reservoirs, and other preemptive uses of the once virgin land. Of the 800,000 acres of forest that once lined the California rivers draining the Sierra Nevada, only 2 percent remains. Twenty percent of what survives stretches along 14 miles of the South Fork of the Kern River as it spills out of **Domeland Wilderness** at the southern terminus of the Sierra Nevada and flows into artificial Lake Isabella to the west. In the Nature Conservancy's four-mile stretch, dense stands of Fremont cottonwood and red willow still shade the river, providing habitat for an amazing number of animals including more than 200 bird species, such as the yellow-billed cuckoo, which the state has listed as threatened.

The preserve lies in a lush, bucolic valley blessed with few people, a temperate climate, and moderate elevation of 2,600 to 2,700 feet. The river passes through the preserve from east to west, and several small irrigation ditches and beaver ponds are scattered about the land. Fertile alluvial soils, a high water table, and ample sunshine foster a healthy forest mixed with thickets of mule-fat, sandbar willow, stinging nettle, and rabbitbrush.

For centuries members of the Tubatalabal tribe roamed this valley, living off its abundant game and plants and leaving grinding holes in the granite boulders at the northwestern edge of the preserve. Shortly after 1850, European settlers began clearing the land for pastures and raised cattle and hay. Agriculture continues to play a major role in the valley, where the Conservancy leases 200 acres of its preserve for cattle grazing and farming and is also doing some farming of its own. Instead of sowing oats and alfalfa, the Conservancy has planted rows and rows of cottonwood and willow saplings in an ambitious program designed to expand the existing riparian forest by as much as 300 acres. The objective is to enhance habitat for yellow-billed cuckoos and other wildlife, including the state's largest population of willow flycatchers, about 40 pairs of which visit the preserve from late April through summer. Yellow-headed and tricolored blackbirds, black-headed and evening grosbeaks, Lawrence's goldfinches, white-throated swifts, four types of wrens, and four kinds of swallows also rely on the river forest for survival. Wood ducks nest in the river's backwaters while brown towhees feed on wild currants along the banks. Black-crowned night herons, blue-winged teal, mallard, pintail, and a host of other birds congregate in the ponds.

Because it is the hub of three overlapping biogeographic provinces, the preserve hosts an unusual mix of wildlife. It is influenced not only by the Sierra Nevada but also by the Central Valley and the Mojave Desert. On the hillsides overlooking the river grow such desert plants as beaver-tail cactus, and saltgrass and native wild ryegrass—two plants closely associated with the valley—grow in the meadows below. One of the more noteworthy species of plants at the preserve is the alkali mariposa lily, which grows in the moist meadows alongside the river at the east end of the preserve and shows its blossoms in May.

Butterflies are also abundant—some 100 different species have been identified within 15 miles of Lake Isabella. The Eunus skipper was believed to be extinct until 81 were found on the preserve, and the San Emigdio blue was another rare find. Mammals of all sizes frequent the preserve: deer, coyotes, beavers, long-tailed weasels, dusky-footed wood rats, and occasionally black bears and mountain lions. Reptiles include

Gilbert's skinks, desert spiny lizards, and western pond turtles, the only turtles native to interior California. From November to February, the turtles hibernate in the mud at the bottom of the ponds.

May is a good time to visit the Kern River Preserve because songbirds are at the peak of migration, wildflowers are in full bloom, and the river is bustling with energy. The self-guided nature trail that begins outside the front door of the visitor center leads to a reforested meadow, where a platform spans a fence erected to protect young trees from trespassing livestock. Here, in the original forest, grow the oldest willows on the property. In May the cottonwoods loose a snowstorm of seeds clumped together in white cottony balls. Conveniently placed boardwalks traverse the wetter areas, which sustain cattails, tule, and wild celery; deeper spots feature azollas, free-floating water ferns. Soloists in the avian harmony include house wrens, song sparrows, plain titmice, and ten kinds of warblers. As the trail winds along the river's edge, gleaming iridescent tree swallows dart over the water to and from their nests in abandoned woodpecker holes. Western woodpewees, hidden from view, call shrilly above the babble of the river.

To get a bird's-eye view of the preserve, head down Sierra Way near the property's western boundary and follow the path that begins on the right side of the road just after the bridge. It parallels the river and passes through a jumble of granite—look for the Indian grinding holes—and across a patch of a type of wild cucumber called manroot, named for its human-sized taproot. The river is quiet here, stilled by the logs felled by beavers. Years ago these toothy mammals were introduced to the high country by the state; eventually they moved downstream and also became established at lower elevations. Follow the trail as it gradually climbs the hill, and above tree level, pull up a rock and share the view with the hawks and falcons that roost in nearby crevices. Trace the length of California's longest intact river forest as it winds out of the mountains, stretches across the valley, and disappears into the lapping waters of the reservoir downstream—a thick green gallery of trees offering hope for hundreds of species of wildlife and future generations.

RIGHT: *Distinguished by its heart-shaped face and long, narrow beak, a common barn owl extends its wing to strike a defensive pose while guarding a nestful of young hidden in the cavity of a tree.*

NORTHERN CALIFORNIA

nch for inch, the northern third of California is the most biologically and geographically diverse region in the state. In an area 11
times the size of Los Angeles County but containing one eighth
of the population are rocky sea-lashed cliffs, steep redwood-
studded coastal mountains, vast fertile valleys, lush river canyons, ice-
capped volcanoes, lifeless lava flows, desolate plateaus, and windswept prairies.

So many radically different landscapes encompass a dizzying spectrum of habitat types. In one 125-mile cross-section as the bald eagle
flies, for example, are hundreds of different animal species, from
California gray whales to pronghorn, from puffins to prairie falcons,
from sea lions to desert striped whipsnakes. Plant life is equally varied.
Northern California's floristic assemblages range from coastal dunes to
cismontane light soil flower fields. Such depth and diversity make even
the most energetic of botanists wonder if there are enough days in a
lifetime to see everything.

Northern California is a far-flung territory, a place where isolated
ranches and scattered small towns dot the landscape. Redding, the
largest city in this 45,000-square-mile region, has a population of only
about 67,000. Natural resources remain the economic mainstay here.

LEFT: *The mists and rains of California's North Coast nurture a temperate
rainforest where evergreens and sword ferns grow tall and thick. Here
denizens of Prairie Creek Redwoods State Park stretch skyward.*

Commercial fishing operations ply the slate-gray waters off the rocky coast for salmon. Loggers work the forests in the rain-drenched coastal mountains. Farmers sow and reap a bounty of crops in the fertile Sacramento Valley. And ranchers wrangle cattle in the northeast corner.

The link between humans and the land extends beyond economic dependence because the natural world is never far from view. Much of this part of the state is national forest, some of it officially designated wilderness. Also occupying large areas are Lassen and Redwood national parks and the sprawling Lava Beds National Monument; the redwoods have been assigned the same international status as the Egyptian pyramids. Along with dozens of state parks, beaches, and recreational areas, there are private nature preserves and several internationally recognized wildlife refuges. The only major undammed river in the state, the Smith, flows here, and no place else on earth boasts taller trees.

Looking north from Sacramento, the topography of northern California is shaped like a giant horseshoe. The Coast Range to the west, the Cascade Range to the north, and the Sierra Nevada to the east ring a flat, open river valley. Running down the middle of this valley, the Sacramento River starts as a bouncing stream, then thickens into a flat slow-moving waterway as it collects runoff from the surrounding mountains. Its mouth, inundated with rising seawater from the retreat of the last Ice Age, is San Francisco Bay. Surrounded by miles of rich bottomland, the river serves as a visual center divider for the millions of waterfowl and other migrant birds traveling the great aerial highway overhead, the Pacific Flyway.

A sometimes misty, sometimes sparkling backdrop at the north end of the Sacramento River Valley is formed by the brooding volcano tops of the Cascade Range. Youthful and impudent, these mountains erupted in the middle of northern California in a cloud of belching black smoke, spewing rivers of red-hot molten rock that stained the land with immense tarlike lava flows. A counterclockwise auto route through this tortured landscape provides visitors with visceral evidence of just how young and restless California's geology is.

OVERLEAF: *Hidden coves and forested headlands are found all along the rocky North Coast. Here Sitka spruce and wild radishes populate the shoreline of Trinidad State Beach near Redwood National Park.*

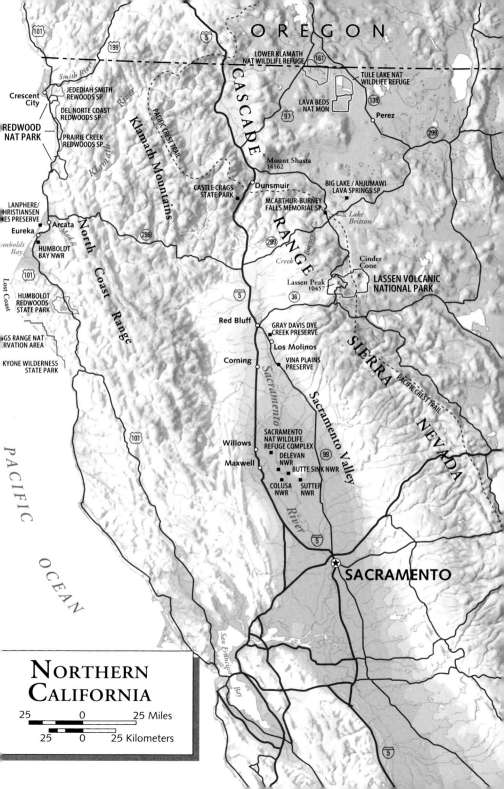

East of the Cascades is an ancient seabed covered with enormous floods of black basalt lava, the desolate and seldom visited Modoc Plateau. To the west is the tangled knot of the Klamath Range, which was originally connected to the Sierra Nevada before being cut off and cast adrift about 140 million years ago, when the rocks were still young and the processes that created them still active.

The mountains to the west of these are younger still. California's northern Coast Range is composed of scrapings from the ocean floor that have been stuck to the edge of the continent much as an artist adds clay to a sculpture. Often clad in fog and mist, this moist marine climate fosters a living laboratory of plants, including the coast redwood, the world's tallest tree. Although its height and girth dwarf the tiny orcutt grass that grows in the Sacramento River Valley, both are native plants, endemic species found naturally nowhere else on earth, testament to northern California's rich and biologically diverse natural heritage.

This chapter's counterclockwise exploration of northern California travels north from Sacramento through the Sacramento River Valley to the Sacramento National Wildlife Refuge Complex and the bubbling mud pots and lakes of Lassen Volcanic National Park. It then heads north into the Cascades to visit the lava tubes and caves of Lava Beds

Waterfowl follow northern California's chain of wetlands as they migrate up and down the Pacific Flyway. Low-flying male northern pintail in tight formation (left) court a hen; the peregrine falcon (top right) nests on ledges and relies on superior speed to pick off prey; and the snowy egret (bottom right), a common sight throughout the Central Valley, shuffles its feet in shallow water to flush small fish and frogs.

National Monument and the teeming Tule Lake and Lower Klamath national wildlife refuges. To survey the majestic coastal redwoods at Redwood National Park, the route swings northwest and follows the coast south as far as the town of Leggett, stopping at a lively dunes preserve and the rugged and seldom visited King Range National Conservation Area.

SACRAMENTO RIVER VALLEY

At 382 miles, the Sacramento is the state's longest river and one of its most important waterways. Born from snowmelt atop the southern Cascade mountains and fed with runoff from the Klamath and North Coast ranges to the west and the northern Sierra Nevada to the east, the mighty river runs south to San Francisco Bay. Along the way it courses through the great valley that bears its name, irrigating the patchwork quilt of rice fields and orchards that blanket the rich, fertile land flanking its banks.

In addition to its vital role in the state's agricultural industry, the Sacramento proves indispensable to wildlife. Anadromous fish such as steelhead trout and salmon depend on it for survival, as do the legions of migratory waterfowl that follow its length as they travel the Pacific Flyway. Countless other species of mammals, amphibians, and reptiles also call the river and adjoining lands home.

Interstate 5 parallels the river, leading about 60 miles north of the state capital to the **Sacramento National Wildlife Refuge Complex❖** near Willows, a 46,425-acre checkerboard of wetland, up-

99

land, and woodland habitats protected by six refuges and three conservation easement areas. The complex is an oasis in a sea of farms.
Beginning in the late 1800s and accelerating in the early 1900s, agriculture replaced natural habitat with rice, wheat, alfalfa, and other
commercial crops. This conversion had a disastrous effect on the millions of ducks, geese, and swans that had relied on the Sacramento
Valley as a key wintering site for thousands of years. To offset the
loss, five preserves starting with the Sacramento Wildlife Refuge in
1937 were created to provide wintering habitat for waterfowl. Next
came the **Delevan❖, Colusa❖, Butte Sink❖,** and **Sutter❖** refuges,
and the sixth, the **Sacramento River Refuge❖,** was added in 1989 to
protect and restore riparian habitat.

More than 300 species of birds and mammals use the refuges at
various times of the year. Between November and February, some 2
million ducks and 500,000 geese may be present at any given time. In
December, for example, visitors can find as many as 200,000 geese on
one refuge. The snow geese have flown from as far away as Wrangel
Island off the coast of Siberia.

Other waterbirds—egrets, avocets, white-faced ibis, and herons—are
common and especially noticeable in spring. Raptors include red-tailed
hawks, northern harriers, black-shouldered kites, and golden eagles.
Lucky visitors may spot bald eagles and endangered peregrine falcons.

All the refuges are easily reached from Interstate 5, and two, Sacramento and Colusa, feature established auto tour routes. Sacramento,
where the complex's headquarters is located, abuts the freeway between the towns of Maxwell and Willows on both sides of Norman
Road. In fall and winter, water is released to create seasonally flooded
marshes where waterfowl rest and feed among cattails, three species
of bulrush, swamp timothy, and smartweed.

Permanent ponds have been created to provide year-round habitat
for locally nesting birds and other resident wildlife. In some areas, wa-
tergrass is irrigated as a natural food source for resident and migrant
waterfowl. Sprangletop, spike rush, millet, Bermuda grass, joint grass,
and smartweed all grow here. In the uplands, saltgrass, saltbush, and
annual grasses offer food and cover for countless wildlife species, including pheasant. After seasonal rains, cackling Canada geese and
wigeon visit to feed on the green sprouts. In spring, vernal pools en-

circled by brilliantly colored concentric rings of goldfield, bluebells, and white popcorn flowers dot the fields.

As it parallels Logan Creek, the refuge's auto route brings visitors face to face with a vital streamside corridor. Although it is the least abundant type on most of the refuges, riparian habitat supports the greatest diversity of wildlife. Wood ducks, hooded mergansers, egrets, great blue herons, owls, beavers, raccoon, and a variety of songbirds dwell among the thick stands of cottonwood and willow.

Farther north on Interstate 5, at the town of Corning, County Road A9 heads east to the Nature Conservancy's **Vina Plains Preserve❖,** just off Route 99. A rarity in the Sacramento Valley, this 1,950-acre patch of annual grassland that has never been plowed still supports a floristic assemblage already extirpated in most other parts of the state. No fewer than 280 species of vascular plants grow here, 6 of them rare: Ahart's paronychia, Hoover's spurge, Greene's tuctoria, hairy orcuttia, slender orcuttia, and adobe lily. Its two distinct plant communities include cismontane light soil flower field and northern basalt vernal pool.

Vina Plains owes its distinctive flora to a rich geologic past. The impervious, rocky hardpan was formed by volcanic mudflows a million or more years ago. Later—about 100,000 years ago—weathering weakened the cementlike conglomerate and converted the rock back to sand, gravel, and eventually clay. Then, 90,000 to 80,000 years later, wind during the glacial period or flooding from the Sacramento River formed sand and silt deposits. Working in concert, strong winds and dry climate removed the upper deposit of soil and scoured vernal pools into the weakened conglomerate.

The underlying impermeable layer of clay causes the vernal pools to fill with rain in winter, and because the pools have no outlet, the water escapes through evaporation. Native plants that have adapted to these special conditions germinate and sprout following summer flooding, blooming in concentric bands of color when the ponds dry. Vernal pools also support a diverse and distinctive array of invertebrates, including snails, insects, and three types of shrimp.

The second plant community is characterized by thin soils that support perennial herbs, annual forbs, and native and introduced grasses. Because the soils produce only a thin cover of grass, the spring display of wildflowers is consistently showier than those in other parts of the state.

101

ABOVE: *Depicted in a nine-teenth-century book illus-tration, Harvest brodiaea, a native of dry plains and grassy hillsides that grows at Vina Plains, sends up its blue violet flowers in early summer.*

From February to May, Vina Plains is ablaze with alternating waves of blooms. Among the more colorful flowering plants are white-flowered navarretia, adobe lilies, Ithuriel's spears, and meadow foam. Almost every conceivable family is represented: crowfoot, mallow, geranium, violet, poppy, mustard, primrose, pea, and snapdragon, to name just a few. Providing a verdant backdrop to the dollops of color are numerous grass species, including meadow foxtail, wild oats, pricklegrass, annual hairgrass, western witchgrass, Pacific bluegrass, and foxtail fescue.

Another unique area managed by the Nature Conservancy is just a short drive north on Route 99, east of the town of Los Molinos on 68th Avenue and then east on Foothill Road. The 37,540-acre **Gray Davis Dye Creek Preserve❖** stretches between the lowlands of the Sacramento River Valley and the foothills of the Cascade Range and the Sierra Nevada. More vernal pools form in its grasslands, and dense riparian vegetation clings to the banks of Dye Creek.

The preserve's most notable feature is an extensive blue oak woodland, one of the best remaining examples of this uniquely Californian vegetation because oak woodlands elsewhere in the state have been cut down to make way for housing subdivisions. The rolling hills, woodlands, streams, and ponds at Dye Creek are wintering grounds for the largest deer herd in California. Also in winter, 25 species of waterfowl visit the preserve's ponds, including tundra swans, great blue herons, and 3 subspecies of Canada geese. As at Vina Plains, access to Dye Creek is permitted on scheduled guided tours only. Visitors must contact the Conservancy's San Francisco office for tour information and reservations.

LASSEN VOLCANIC NATIONAL PARK

North of the Sacramento River Valley, the flat terrain gives way to the ruggedly mountainous Cascade Range, which extends 500 miles north through Oregon and Washington to British Columbia. In California, the snow-capped peaks are interspersed with river valleys, high plateaus, and lifeless lava flows.

From Route 99 north near Red Bluff, head east on Route 36, then north on Route 89 to the southwestern entrance of **Lassen Volcanic National Park❖.** The peak that gives the park its name is actually the southernmost volcano in a chain of 16 that form a segment of the great volcanic Ring of Fire encircling the Pacific Ocean. Lassen Peak is also one of the most recently active. Earlier in this century, the park literally exploded into being when the volcano blew its top, sending a tower of smoke and ash 25,000 to 40,000 feet into the stratosphere.

Geologically speaking, the story really began 70 million years ago, when the entire western portion of the continent became subject to profound earth movements. Gradually, over millions of years, the rocks of the earth's crust were folded and fractured, permitting lava to rise to the surface. Volcanoes burst into activity, piling lava and ash on top of one another and forming the Cascades.

ABOVE: *Snake lily, or twining brodiaea— recorded in this stylized vintage illustration— clambers through shrubbery at the Nature Conservancy's Vina Plains Preserve.*

About 600,000 years ago, in the park's southwest corner, a giant stratovolcano, Mount Tehama, gradually rose through countless eruptions to 11,000 feet. Eventually, glaciation and hydrothermal alteration caused it to collapse along a series of fault lines crisscrossing it. About 30,000 years ago, however, lava began to rise from a vent on Tehama's north slope, creating Lassen Peak, among the world's largest plug-dome volcanoes.

103

For the next several thousand years volcanic activity remained sporadic, but in 1914 the eruptions became more frequent. On May 15, 1915, the volcano exploded in a powerful blast, creating volcanic mudflows that poured down a thousand feet toward the Sacramento River Valley a few days later. On May 22, a great explosion rocked the peak, blasting out a new crater, flattening trees a mile in each direction, and sending high into the sky a huge black mushroom cloud filled with steam and rock fragments that cast a pall for miles. So large was the cloud, in fact, that it could be seen from the cupola of the state capitol in Sacramento more than 150 miles away.

That supreme effort exhausted Lassen, and with the exception of occasional bursts of steam, the peak has been quiet since 1921. Still, visitors in search of vulcanism won't be disappointed because Lassen's violent legacy is visible at every turn.

From the southwestern entrance, Route 89 winds through a tortured landscape of hardscrabble slopes and crumbling rock faces that are the remains of the Tuscan formation, a precursor to the later Mount Tehama. The volcanic rocks are all varieties of andesite and dacite, the most common kinds of rock in volcanic chains. Andesites come in a spectrum of grays, browns, and reds, whereas dacites appear in somewhat lighter shades.

Not to be missed are Bumpass Hell and Supan Springs at the **Sulphur Works,** two groups of volcanic hot springs, gas vents, bubbling mud pots, and steaming fumaroles created by surface water seeping downward through cracks, heating on bodies of hot rock a few hundred feet underground, and boiling back to the surface. When it emerges into the air and cools, the highly mineralized water leaves behind alienlike structures of siliceous sinter and white travertine. Following the boardwalks among bubbling mud pots and through thick clouds of steam is like walking across a giant cauldron of stew.

Winding up the slopes of Eagle and Lassen peaks, the road passes **Emerald Lake,** a remnant of glacial erosion. The park was covered by ice and snow during the last Ice Age, and the valleys below the

RIGHT: *Crossing a vast lava plateau, a hiker sets out to explore Cinder Cone and the Painted Dunes at Lassen Volcanic National Park. The southernmost Cascades volcano, Lassen erupted violently in 1915.*

peaks were scoured clean. Along the highest part of the road, beautiful sections of solid lava lie exposed.

At 7,000-foot-high Summit Lake, intrepid visitors can leave their cars and set out on foot. One of the most scenic portions of the park's 150 miles of hiking trails connects Summit and Butte lakes. Along the way, it passes a chain of pristine glacial lakes, crosses the famous Pacific Crest Trail, traverses the pastel Painted Dunes overlooking the chunky black Fantastic Lava Beds, and encircles Cinder Cone, a 6,907-foot volcanic mount produced 1,500 years ago by a series of violent eruptions. Dusting the area for 30 square miles, volcanic debris spewed from its top, and the ash from its fumaroles fell on nearby streams, creating the Painted Dunes. Cinder Cone belched its last in 1851. That year, an unusual basaltic lava flow was extruded from the cone's flank.

ABOVE: *In spring a pair of red fox kits frolic by their den; by four months these timid, normally nocturnal omnivores are on their own.*

LEFT: *Clouds of steam spew from volcanic hot springs and gas vents at Bumpass Hell in Lassen's Sulphur Works area; boardwalks lead visitors through the vaporous fumaroles.*

Continuing north, Route 89 passes the Devastated Area, where earth's green mantle of plants is slowly but relentlessly covering the layers of volcanic debris. Although Lassen Park is primarily known for its vulcanism, in a rich diversity of plant and animal life more than 700 flowering plant species provide food and shelter for 250 vertebrates and a host of invertebrates.

Lassen owes its abundant flora and fauna to its setting at the crossroads of three great biological provinces: the Cascades to the north, the Sierra Nevada to the south, and the Great Basin Desert to the east. A mixed conifer forest of ponderosa pine, incense cedar, sugar pine, white fir, and Douglas fir growing in the lower-elevation Transition zone is home to such birds as common flickers, olive-sided flycatchers, western wood-pewees, great horned owls, and pileated woodpeckers. Just above lies the upper montane forest, or Canadian zone, where red fir predominates among less diverse vegetation. Animal species include

ABOVE: *Floating on slender stems above feathery grasses, the sleek blossoms of mountain shooting star resemble small speeding rockets.*
RIGHT: *At McArthur–Burney Falls, visitors can hear the thundering cascades long before they can see the spectacular plume of water.*

Williamson's sapsuckers, hermit thrushes, red foxes, and pine marten.

Even higher is the subalpine, or Hudsonian, zone, where the trees—whitebark pine and mountain hemlock—are gnarled from harsh winter snows and fierce winds. Their prostrate position, dwarf growth habit, and gnarled appearance mark them as *krummholz,* meaning "crooked wood" in German. Bare patches of ground alternate with the wooded areas. In this zone, abundant sun and moisture nurture a large number of shrubs and wildflowers, including red heather, rock spirea, King's sandwort, Sierra pincushion, pioneer rock cress, and Lyall's lupine. Common birds are Clark's nutcrackers and mountain chickadees, and mammals include yellow-bellied marmots and pikas. The highest vegetation zone at Lassen is the alpine community, where plant life is restricted to ground-hugging pussytoes, golden draba, alpine sorrel, and dwarf hulsea. Gray-crowned rosy finches live here, and the only mammals to be seen are the ubiquitous pikas.

THE CASCADES

Heading north from Lassen, Route 89 leads to **McArthur–Burney Falls Memorial State Park❖.** Called the eighth wonder of the world by President Theodore Roosevelt, Burney Falls cascades 129 feet over a black volcanic cliff garlanded with tropical-looking vegetation. Even more impressive is the sheer volume of water—100 million gallons—roaring over the falls every day. Smaller falls seep from the broad-faced cliff, creating a curtain of feathery water on either side of the main plume.

Nesting on the steep cliff face are black swifts and swallows, and the deep canyon below shelters belted kingfishers, owls, woodpeckers, many species of songbirds, squirrels, and skunks. The 800-acre park stretches two miles down Burney Creek to the mouth of nine-mile-long Lake Britton. Double-crested cormorants, pied-billed grebes, and nesting bald eagles can be seen fishing the lake's open waters while great blue herons and many species of ducks feed along the oak-shaded shore.

ABOVE: *Splattered like mud but twice as hard, the rocks atop Hippo Butte provide a panorama of the once-molten terrain at Lava Beds National Monument; volcanoes were active here for one million years.*

Return south on Route 89, head east on Route 299, and then turn north on McArthur's Main Street and follow the signs to **Big Lake–Ahjumawi Lava Springs State Park❖.** Big Lake, a popular fishing spot owned by the Pacific Gas and Electric Company, provides boat access to the open grasslands, forested hills, and rugged lava flows of the wildlife-rich state park behind it. Geese, swans, and ducks are drawn to the lake and adjacent fields. Herons have built a rookery in the pine trees east of Crystal Springs while ospreys nest in the tops of junipers. Mule deer, coyotes, and yellow-bellied marmots dwell in the forest too.

Continue east on Route 299 to Route 139, turning north at Conby for 26 miles to the signed road to **Lava Beds National Monument❖.** Within its 47,000 acres, visitors can find cinder cones, spatter cones, chimneys, and immense flows of lava—both pahoehoe (smooth and ropy) and 'a'a (rough and jagged).

Surely the biggest attraction is the network of lava tubes underlying the monument like tunnels in a prairie-dog community. The tubes were formed when rivers of 1,800-degree-Fahrenheit lava pouring out of vents and craters cooled on the outside while continuing to flow hot and fast inside. When the eruptions stopped, so did the rivers of lava,

Above: *A scenic drive links the most accessible of the more than 200 caves and grottoes at Lava Beds. In Fern Cave, paintings by the ancient Modoc people cover the walls and can be visited with permission.*

leaving behind tunnels or tubes—some more than a mile long. As they cooled, portions of the lava tubes' roofs collapsed, and the rain, plants, and animals that ventured in have created their own world.

Near the visitor center just past the southeast entrance, Cave Loop Road provides access to a dozen of the most prominent of the monument's 200-plus caves and grottoes. Mushpot Cave, equipped with lights and signs explaining the various formations, offers a good introduction for the beginning spelunker. Nearby Labyrinth and Lava Brook caves, connected by a hip-hugging passageway, feature frothy pahoehoe, lava pillars and benches, and "lavacicles." Extensive yellowish deposits of bacteria, which turn to gold when covered with water droplets, give Golden Dome Cave its name. Likewise, pale powder-blue bacteria on the ceiling distinguish the Blue Grotto.

Lava Beds is rich in cultural history as well. The sagebrush-covered lava plateaus and wooded mountains were once home to the Modoc, Native Americans who subsisted on fish, waterfowl, wild game, seeds, and bulbs. In the 1800s, white settlers moving into the area demanded that the U.S. Army remove the Modoc from their homes. The Modoc resisted relocation to a reservation near Klamath Falls, Oregon, and the

111

only U.S. Army general ever killed in an Indian war died in the ensuing skirmish. Led by a charismatic chief named Captain Jack, some of the Modoc fled to a lava stronghold in the present-day monument. Eventually the army tracked them down, hanged Captain Jack, and sent most of the rest of the tribe to a reservation in Oklahoma where disease largely accomplished what bullets could not.

Although the Modocs and their civilization are gone from the area, one of their principal game animals remains. Virtually extirpated throughout California, a tiny herd of pronghorn hangs on in the eastern portion of the monument. The shy, elusive animals are best observed in early morning or late evening as they feed on grass and sagebrush. When spooked, they flee across the windswept plateau at speeds up to 40 miles per hour. Other species sharing the sagebrush-covered terrain include golden-mantled ground squirrels, kangaroo rats, yellow-bellied marmots, jackrabbits, California quail, and meadowlarks. Along the cliffs, look for bald eagles and 24 species of hawks, falcons, owls, and other birds of prey.

More birds can be found at the monument's neighbor to the north, **Tule Lake National Wildlife Refuge❖,** and the nearby **Lower Klamath National Wildlife Refuge❖,** which are part of a six-refuge complex designed to protect wildlife habitats in the Klamath Basin. Prior to the 1900s, the Klamath Basin was composed of large shallow lakes and extensive marshes—an immense wetland habitat for untold thousands of shorebirds and fall peak populations of six million waterfowl. Earlier in this century, most of the basin's marshes were diked and drained and converted to agriculture. Alarmed by these changes, President Theodore Roosevelt established the Lower Klamath as the

nation's first waterfowl refuge in 1908. Tule Lake received protected status 20 years later.

Together, the two refuges encompass 86,500 acres of mostly open water, marsh, upland, and cropland. On the land where farmers are permitted to grow grain and potatoes, crop leftovers provide feed for birds. The combination of open water and abundant food attracts enormous flocks of migratory waterfowl, including snow geese, cackling Canada geese, northern pintail, and American wigeon. Species such as prairie falcons, Ross's geese, and American white pelicans are also found here. The 200 species of breeding birds include western grebes, cinnamon teal, and threatened greater sandhill cranes. The two refuges—whose diversity has made them internationally famous—also boast the largest concentration of wintering bald eagles outside Alaska.

Visitors can tour the refuges on self-guided auto routes. The roads—actually improved dikes—are easy to drive and pass a variety of habitat types, allowing close-up views of numerous species. A special attraction of the Tule Lake refuge is a marked canoe trail through two miles of quiet water channels within a 2,500-acre hard-stem bulrush–cattail marsh. From a canoe, paddlers can spot dozens of marsh-dwelling

113

species, including black-crowned night herons, white-faced ibis, common yellowthroats, soras, Virginia rail, lesser scaup, and ring-billed gulls.

Route 161 cuts across the top of the Lower Klamath refuge and dead-ends into Route 97. Heading southwest, Route 97 intersects Interstate 5 south to complete the tour of the Cascades. An excellent spot to appreciate the magnificence of this volcanic range is **Castle Crags State Park❖,** just south of the town of Dunsmuir on the west side of I-5. Here granite spires, towering pillars, and sheer cliff faces resemble the picturesque ruins of a mythical fortress. That the jagged landscape is a granitic intrusion reminiscent of those in the Sierra Nevada is no coincidence, because Castle Crags belongs to the Klamath Mountains, a poorly understood range that geologists believe was connected to the Sierra Nevada, 60 miles to the east. The two blocks were separated about 140 million years ago when the Klamaths moved west and an ancient seaway gap formed between them. Later, this gap was partially filled by the southern terminus of the Cascade Range.

ABOVE: *Related to the rabbit, the pika is a small, social creature that lives in large colonies high on talus slopes and communicates in shrill nasal bleats.*

RIGHT: *Looming above Douglas fir forests and clearings full of blooming lupine are the rugged spires and sheer cliffs that give Castle Crags State Park its name.*

Castle Crags features a 5.5-mile trail that leads visitors through thick forests of ponderosa pine, Douglas fir, incense cedar, and black oak. As Steller's jays, red-shafted flickers, and woodpeckers fill the forest with song, look for mule deer, black bears, mountain lions, mink, and river otters. From a vantage point atop the Crags, visitors can look northeast to the gleaming outline of one of the Cascade's crown jewels, **Mount Shasta,** a now-dormant volcano that instills a sense of awe and wonder at the powerful forces that shaped this land.

NORTH COAST

West of the Cascade and Klamath ranges lies a group of mountains known collectively as the North Coast Range. These coastal mountains

are composed of layers of muddy sediment scraped off the floor of the ocean and stuck onto the edge of the continent as the Pacific plate was being subducted beneath the North American plate. Similar in appearance to western Oregon and Washington, California's north coast is a temperate rain forest. In this cool, moist climate, fog is frequent, even in summer, and rain is measured in feet, not inches. The abundant precipitation nurtures thick stands of evergreens that run from mountaintop to shoreline. Among them grow the tallest trees in the world, the coast redwoods.

These towering giants are direct descendants of a species that dates back to the Age of Dinosaurs. Once found throughout the Northern Hemisphere, redwood habitat shrank as climate changed. By the time European settlers arrived in the West, only two species of redwood remained, the giant sequoia in small pockets in the Sierra Nevada and the coast redwood along a narrow strip of Pacific coast in northern California and southwestern Oregon. Of the two, the coastal variety is the taller and thinner.

116

LEFT: *A pinyon-juniper woodland dotted by yellow-flowered rabbitbrush gives way to the snow-covered slopes of Mount Shasta, a 14,000-foot volcanic peak in the Cascade Range that last erupted in 1786.*

The advent of mechanized logging reduced the coast redwood's range even further. In less than 150 years, nearly 2 million acres of coast redwood habitat was lost, and today only 135,000 acres remain. Much of that survives in a 50-mile stretch south of Crescent City along Route 101. **Redwood National Park❖** was formed by an act of Congress in 1968 and enlarged ten years later. A United Nations–designated International Biosphere Reserve and World Heritage Site, this 110,232-acre park encompasses federal land as well as three state parks.

The redwood groves along the north coast are a prime example of old-growth forest, a vital ecosystem that features old and young trees growing together, a mixture essential to the genetic diversity and health of a forest. The older trees are 250 to 1,000 years old (a coast redwood can live 2,000 years). From 200 to 300 feet tall with trunks up to 22 feet in diameter, coast redwoods are typically covered with a thick growth of moss and lichen that harbor many species of insects, birds, and small mammals. Their gargantuan trunks store thousands of gallons of water, and their 12-inch-thick bark protects them from fire, disease, and insects.

Often the tops of the old-growth trees have been sheared off by wind or lightning, leaving cavities that such birds as endangered northern spotted owls use as nests. Alive or dead, the big trees support life. Large dead snags may remain erect for more than 200 years, providing food for insects and woodpeckers and habitat for other species. In turn, these creatures become food for larger predators, such as marten and black bears. Fallen trees help hold steep soils in place, and in the 500

OVERLEAF: *The dim, moist understory of mist-enshrouded Del Norte Coast Redwoods State Park is brightened by the pink and red flowers of the California rosebay, a rhododendron native to the coast.*

years a big tree may take to decay, dozens of insect, bird, and mammal species will use it for shelter or food. This biological activity creates in the rotting wood greater concentrations of nutrients like phosphorus and nitrogen, which in turn feed the roots of nearby living trees.

Jedediah Smith Redwoods State Park❖ is nine miles east of Crescent City on Route 199. Named for the first European to travel overland from the Mississippi River to California and to cross the Sierra Nevada, the park protects one of the finest redwood groves in the state in its 9,500 acres. Although the trees are impressive, the real attraction here is the wild and free-flowing Smith River, the only major river in California without a dam. A mecca for anglers, it holds the state record for steelhead trout—a 27-pounder. Along the banks, mist-shrouded trees form a canopy over a rich, verdant forest floor brightened by white, red, and shocking-pink rhododendrons.

At **Del Norte Coast Redwoods State Park❖,** beginning seven miles south of Crescent City via Route 101, second-growth redwoods, planted early in this century, frame a spectacularly scenic coastline. With stretches of steep, rocky cliffs broken by rolling slopes, redwood country's rugged coastline deserves protected status simply for itself. In December and May, visitors on promontories can see California gray whales migrating between their breeding grounds in the Gulf of California and the Arctic. Sea lions feed beyond the surf and haul out on sea stacks (offshore rocks). Murres, double-crested cormorants, puffins, auklets, several species of gulls, and pigeon guillemots nest in sea cliffs.

Prairie Creek Redwoods State Park❖, south of the Klamath River on Route 101, is the most diverse of the three state parks within the Redwood National Park group. Within its bounds are 70 miles of hiking trails, redwood forests, flat-bottom canyons, ocean beaches, and open meadows. The park is also home to a large herd of Roosevelt elk, handsome creatures that can weigh more than a thousand pounds and are distinguished by antlers larger than those of a deer.

Just south, in the federally owned part of the park, is the **Tall Trees Trail,** a moderately steep three-mile round-trip trail that leads to the tallest known tree in the world—a 367.8-foot beauty. The giant grows on the banks of Redwood Creek, a peaceful river in summer, but dangerous to cross in winter. Another popular hike is the easy one-mile loop through **Lady Bird Johnson Grove** among trees more than 300 feet tall and 2,000 years old on a soft carpet of shamrocklike redwood sorrel and "goosepens," the hollowed-out bases of redwoods struck by lightening. Rhododendrons and giant sword ferns lend the forest a tropical air while chestnut-backed chickadees, purple finches, black phoebes, and white-crowned sparrows fill it with song.

Farther south on Route 101 near Arcata is the **Manila Beach and Dunes❖.** Although coastal dunes have disappeared beneath housing tracts and dune-buggy tracks, a thriving remnant holds fast on a narrow sand spit stretching between the Pacific Ocean and Humboldt Bay.

From the entrance to the preserve, a well-marked trail leads through a tunnel in the trees onto a drift of sand bleached white as bone and ribbed by wind-carved furrows. In spring and summer, tenacious wildflowers turn the lunar 80-foot-high dunes into seas of color. Blooming in large, defiant clumps are evening primroses, morning glories, seaside daisies, and a relatively abundant population of Menzies wallflowers, rare and endangered members of the mustard family that grow in only six other locations in the state.

At ocean's edge, the trail follows a spit of driftwood-studded sand before leading back across the dunes toward a forest. A thousand years ago, Wiyot Indians camped on the dunes and lived off fish and clams they took from the ocean and mudflats and rabbits and quail they hunted in the forests. Occasionally the wind uncovers one of their ancient shell middens, long-forgotten refuse heaps containing stone sinkers used for fishing nets, spear and arrow points, and knives and drills.

Beneath the trees in a thick stand of Sitka spruce and beach pine lies a blanket of miniature manzanita (known as bearberry) and reindeer lichen—two species of the Arctic tundra that migrated south during climatic cooling and survived subsequent warming trends in this moderate marine environment. White as snow, the lichen grows in dense, spongy patches in winter and dies in summer.

In the forest, a veritable greenhouse for plants, several different types of orchids thrive, including ladies' tresses, calypso, rein orchid, and rattlesnake-plantain. More than 200 species of fungi are also found here, among them at least 23 types new to science, new to California, or new to North America. In the fall, millions of mushrooms splashed red, yellow, purple, and lavender transform the forest into a mycologist's paradise.

The abundant flora supports a healthy population of fauna. Gray foxes make dens in the dense cover of huckleberry and willow while striped skunks, porcupines, raccoon, bobcats, and long-tailed weasels forage nearby. The more than 200 species of birds identified include the curious-looking red crossbill. Males garbed in brick-red plumes cling to pine cones, noisily extracting seeds with their peculiar bills clearly crossed at the tip. The tallest trees are perches for 15 species of raptors, including owls and falcons, and at dusk, great blue herons return from a day's hunting in the salt marshes to roost in the spruces.

Slightly farther south, via Route 101 11 miles south of Eureka, are additional colonies of water birds at the **Humboldt Bay National Wildlife Refuge❖.** The 2,200-acre preserve—consisting of diked marshes, seasonal wetlands, salt marshes, mudflats, and open water—contains the largest eelgrass beds in the state, a vital spring staging area for black brant. Visitors can see more than 25,000 of these marine geese at a time as they feed in the eelgrass beds at low tide and raft up in large groups on the open water during high tide. Huge flocks of western sandpipers, dunlins, curlews, and willet scurry along the shore while American bitterns, herons, and egrets wade along Salmon Creek and Hookton Slough. Songbirds congregate in the adjacent grasslands in spring.

ABOVE: *Symbol of the conflict between environmentalists and loggers, the northern spotted owl faces extinction as old-growth habitat disappears.*

More groves of coast redwood are protected at **Humboldt Redwoods State Park❖,** 45 miles south of Eureka on Route 101. Within its 51,000 acres, this often-bypassed park contains a singularly impressive stand of redwood—the **Rockefeller Forest.** A five-mile road winds through this matchless 10,000-acre grove, and hikers can take to the 100-mile network of trails to explore an additional 7,000 acres of old-growth redwood in the park.

LEFT: *Greens of every hue tint the mosses and ferns that thrive in a thick tangle of vegetation in Prairie Creek Redwoods State Park.*

123

LEFT: *Colorful and just as fragrant as its eastern relative, a western azalea (Rhododendron occidentale) blooms in the Azalea State Reserve just north of Arcata. This shrub thrives in northern California along the coast's moist, forested stream banks.*

RIGHT: *Douglas' irises, named for a nineteenth-century Scottish naturalist also commemorated by the Douglas fir, color the foreground at Trinidad State Beach, a scenic cove of black sand beaches and tree-covered sea stacks.*

The park also boasts one of the greatest drives in the world, the incredibly scenic **Avenue of the Giants.** This 32-mile parkway paralleling Route 101 is hemmed in on all sides by massive trees whose trunks are two to three times as big around as a car. Under a canopy so dense that the road is in perpetual shadow grow sword ferns whose Turkish scimitar–length blades wave in all directions. To experience the grandeur of the park, stop at a pullout and take a short walk back to an age when dinosaurs stalked the earth and primeval forests covered the land. Stand beside one of the towering giants and listen as its sheer size and majesty speak louder than words.

At the south end of the park near Redway, Briceland–Thorne Road heads west toward one of most isolated places in the state, California's aptly named Lost Coast. This extremely steep and rocky terrain is one of the few sections of the 1,100-mile-long coastline that does not have a highway running parallel to it. The only roads that penetrate the rugged landscape are gravel or dirt.

Much of the Lost Coast is administered by the U.S. Bureau of Land Management. The **King Range National Conservation Area**❖ extends some 35 miles between the Mattole River and Whale Gulch and up to 6 miles inland from the Pacific Ocean. A spectacular meeting of

land and sea, the King Range rises from sea level to 4,087 feet at the summit of Kings Peak in less than three miles. The western slope is furrowed by short, steep streams that empty directly into the ocean. Steep slopes, heavy rainfall, and unstable soil and rock formations have created many cliffs, huge rock slides, and talus piles.

Touring the King Range is a challenge. Although a network of gravel and dirt roads serves the experienced four-wheel-drive sightseer, the most sensible way to explore is on foot. A wilderness beach path called the Lost Coast Trail leads to an abandoned Coast Guard lighthouse, relics of early shipwrecks, and shell middens (refuse heaps) left by the area's first inhabitants, the Sinkyone and Mattole Indians. The trail also offers hikers close encounters with resident wildlife. Old-growth forests of Douglas fir provide important habitat for such sensitive species as the northern spotted owl, Cooper's hawk, and bald eagle, while offshore rocks, kelp beds, and tidal areas are home to harbor seals, sea lions, and a variety of seabirds.

Adjoining the conservation area to the south is **Sinkyone Wilderness State Park❖,** a 7,000-acre preserve also designed with the hiker and backpacker in mind. The varied terrain includes three small groves of coast redwoods, old-growth Douglas fir forests, grasslands, coastal bluffs, beaches, and tidal pools—all of which support an equally diverse array of wildlife. A herd of Roosevelt elk was introduced here from Prairie Creek State Park to replace those killed off in the late-nineteenth century, and other resident mammals include black bears, mountain lions, deer, foxes, squirrels, and porcupines. Bird-watchers can look inland for western wood-pewees, Say's phoebes, western kingbirds, violet-green swallows, Anna's hummingbirds, and golden-crowned kinglets. Along the coast, black turnstones, western sandpipers, long-billed dowitchers, common murres, pelagic cormorants, and brown pelicans keep binoculars turning.

Although it may indeed warrant the sobriquet Lost Coast, this part of northern California is sure to be a find in anyone's book.

LEFT: *Despite a devastating lightning strike, a giant redwood tree at Humboldt Redwoods State Park remains alive, nourished by its trunk.* OVERLEAF: *Visitors look for migrating gray whales from North Coast headlands, such as these above the rock-strewn beach at Juan Creek.*

127

THE CALIFORNIA COAST

M ost people's image of the California landscape is the one created by Hollywood: sun, sand, surf, and endless summer. Although celluloid's vision is often distorted, the beach is indeed synonymous with California. By far the majority of state residents live within earshot of the pounding Pacific, drawn, perhaps, by a human need to remain close to their primordial birthplace. The 1,100-mile coastline, where scenery seems to change at every milepost, is also the Golden State's biggest tourist attraction.

Many who visit are surprised to discover how varied California's spectacular shoreline is. Although it borders the same ocean for its entire length, the land comprises many distinctive habitats, ranging from the temperate rain forests of the north to the arid, desertlike beaches of the south. This veritable variety pack of biological diversity is evident in the hundreds of different plant communities that thrive in sea spray. Redwood forests yield to dwarf pines that change to grassy headlands that give way to coastal sage scrub that becomes salt marshes. In turn, each supports a signature assemblage of fauna. Tens of thousands of species of insects and other invertebrates, amphibians, reptiles, fish, birds, and mammals—many occurring nowhere else on the planet—call coastal California home.

LEFT: *Only hearty coastal plants such as ice plant, a nonnative succulent species, survive on the rocky headlands of Channel Islands National Park. The view is of Inspiration Point on East Anacapa Island.*

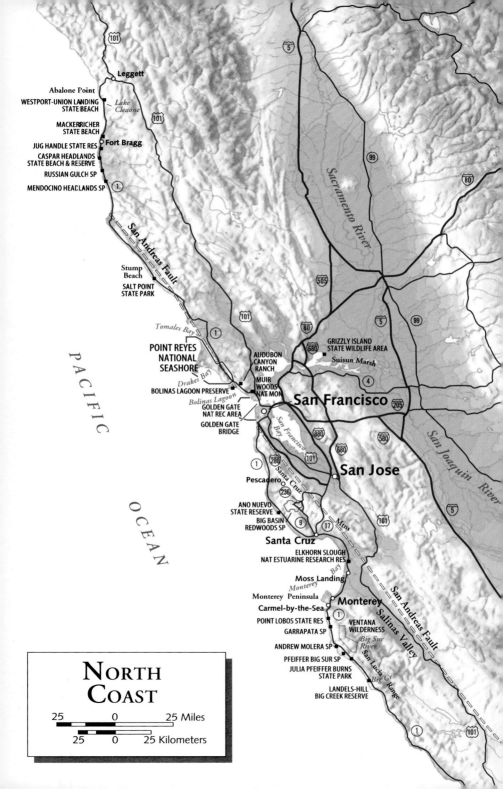

101

Leggett

Abalone Point
WESTPORT-UNION LANDING
STATE BEACH

Lake Cleone

101

MACKERRICHER
STATE BEACH

JUG HANDLE STATE RES
CASPAR HEADLANDS
STATE BEACH & RESERVE
RUSSIAN GULCH SP

MENDOCINO HEADLANDS SP

Fort Bragg

1

San Andreas Fault

Stump
Beach
SALT POINT
STATE PARK

Tomales Bay

1

101

POINT REYES
NATIONAL
SEASHORE

Drakes Bay

AUDUBON
CANYON
RANCH

MUIR
WOODS
NAT MON

BOLINAS LAGOON PRESERVE

Bolinas Lagoon

GOLDEN GATE
NAT REC AREA

GOLDEN GATE
BRIDGE

San Francisco Bay

5

99

80

Sacramento River

505

5

99

80

80

580

GRIZZLY ISLAND
STATE WILDLIFE AREA

Suisun Marsh

4

San Francisco

205

880

San Jose

580

San Joaquin River

1

280

San Bruno Mtns

101

Pescadero

236

Santa Cruz Mtns

ANO NUEVO
STATE RESERVE

BIG BASIN
REDWOODS SP

9

17

Mtns

101

5

Santa Cruz

ELKHORN SLOUGH
NAT ESTUARINE RESEARCH RES

Moss Landing

Monterey Bay

Monterey Peninsula

Carmel-by-the-Sea

POINT LOBOS STATE RES

GARRAPATA SP

ANDREW MOLERA SP

PFEIFFER BIG SUR SP

JULIA PFEIFFER BURNS
STATE PARK

LANDELS-HILL
BIG CREEK RESERVE

Monterey

1

VENTANA
WILDERNESS

Big Sur
River

San Andreas Fault

Salinas Valley

San Lucia Range

Big Sur

101

1

PACIFIC

OCEAN

NORTH
COAST

25   0   25 Miles

25   0   25 Kilometers

25   0   25 Miles

25   0   25 Kilometers

San Andreas Fault

Sierra Madre Mountains

Tehachapi Mountains

Mojave Desert

San Andreas Fault

Transverse Range

Santa Ynez Mtns

San Luis Obispo Bay

Pismo Beach

PISMO STATE BEACH

NIPOMO DUNES PRESERVE

Las Cruces

Santa Barbara

Ventura

Santa Monica Mtns

Oxnard

Anacapa I

SANTA MONICA MTNS NAT REC AREA

San Miguel I

Santa Cruz I

Santa Rosa I

CHANNEL ISLANDS NATIONAL PARK & NATIONAL MARINE SANCTUARY

Los Angeles

Santa Ana Mtns

UPPER NEWPORT BAY ECOLOGICAL RESERVE

San Clemente

Santa Barbara I

San Nicolas I

Santa Catalina I

C H A N N E L

I S L A N D S

San Clemente I

LOS PENASQUITOS LAGOON / TORREY PINES STATE RESERVE

Del Mar

San Diego

TIJUANA RIVER NAT ESTUARINE RESEARCH RESERVE

P A C I F I C

O C E A N

ABOVE: *The setting sun casts a golden glow over sky, sea, and sand at Pfeiffer Beach on the central California coast. The picturesque Big Sur*

The land along the California coast is as restless as the sea it fronts. Powerful forces all but unimaginable in human terms continue to shape it as two huge jigsaw-puzzle pieces of the earth's crust battle to fit together. The resulting collision has created a crumpled landscape of crushed and folded seafloor pushed skyward and exposed to wind, rain, and waves. Four distinct mountain ranges abut the ocean in California, forming a like number of geomorphic provinces. In the north, the North and South Coast ranges rise like colossal bookends flanking San Francisco Bay. In the south, the ranges are the Transverse and Peninsular.

Different ocean currents on either side of the state's coastal "elbow" at Point Conception (40 miles northwest of Santa Barbara) create the distinct climates of north and south. In the north, the ocean current circulates colder water offshore, causing cold and wet weather. South of Point Conception, the shore angles sharply eastward, forming the relatively shallower southern California Bight. The indentation causes slightly warmer water to circulate, directly affecting the temperature onshore.

Despite its many disparate parts, a single ribbon of blacktop binds the California coast together. Starting in the north in Mendocino County, fabled Route 1 winds through redwood forests, over grassy headlands, along rocky coves, and beside deserted beaches. The few towns that

shoreline is renowned for its crashing surf, rocky sea stacks, world-class clouds, steep coastal cliffs—and spectacular sunsets.

dot this region are either small fishing villages at the mouths of rivers pouring down from the Coast Range or former "dog-hole" ports—tiny coves just big enough for "a dog to turn around in" that were ersatz harbors for nineteenth-century schooners carrying redwood lumber.

Just north of San Francisco, a finger of land splits off from the continent, pried apart by the famous San Andreas fault, which curves back into shore here before exiting again at Tomales Bay. Thick forests cover this newly made peninsula, protected as Point Reyes National Seashore. Despite its urban surroundings, San Francisco Bay, the largest estuary in the continental United States, is an important refuge for wildlife.

South of San Francisco, redwood trees tower on the slopes of the Santa Cruz Mountains while huge northern elephant seals roar on a tiny islet offshore. Curving a few miles south is Monterey Bay, home to a submarine gorge deeper than the Grand Canyon. Proposals to confer national park protection on the wild, rugged Big Sur coastline are as perennial as the fog that rolls in each summer to cover the hillsides and steep cliffs rising above the Pacific.

Off the southern coast lie a chain of wild and undeveloped islands where an Ice Age race of pygmy mammoths rest their weary bones. Onshore, native habitat has mostly disappeared beneath the commingling sprawls of Los Angeles and San Diego, but a few pockets still hold fast thanks to a series of hard-won parks and wildlife refuges.

To visit the endlessly varied terrain of the California coast, this chapter takes Route 1 from the northern California town of Leggett and follows the coast south to the Mexican border. Highlights of the trip include the dunes and dramatic headlands of the Mendocino area, the diverse habitats and wildlife of the Point Reyes National Seashore, Muir Woods National Monument, and tortuous forms of Monterey cypresses at Point Lobos State Reserve, the state parks of Big Sur, and the Guadalupe–Nipomo Dunes Preserve. Beckoning along the south coast are the Channel Islands, the rare trees of the Torrey Pines State Reserve, and the abundant bird life of the Tijuana River National Estuarine Research Reserve.

MENDOCINO COUNTY

The coastline of Mendocino County is world-famous for its breathtaking scenery and abundant plant and animal life. Redwood and pine forests line lush river valleys. Small, picturesque towns built on grassy headlands look as though they were plucked from the New England coast. And on every side is the sea, the always changing, ever beautiful sea.

A cluster of state beaches and parks dot the magnificent stretch of coastline south of the junction of Routes 101 and 1 at Leggett. At **Westport–Union Landing State Beach❖,** site of an 1800s schooner landing, a bluff-top campground overlooks a beach where steam-powered sailing ships once anchored to take on redwood lumber. The boards were transported to the ship via a rickety chute suspended over the water by steel cables attached to platforms atop the sea cliff. Endangered Mendocino coast paintbrush grows in a narrow strip of marine terrace above the sea, and at Abalone Point, western gulls, Brandt's and pelagic cormorants, and pigeon guillemots nest on the rocky cliffs.

A few miles farther south on Route 1, **MacKerricher State Park❖** spans eight miles of seashore, gentle lowlands, and several square miles of sand dunes that pose a surprising contrast to the otherwise rocky and often forbidding coastline in these parts. The centerpiece of this 1,600-acre park is **Lake Cleone,** a tidal lagoon that was closed off from the ocean in the 1940s by a now-abandoned road. Stocked with rainbow trout, it is popular among anglers and among dabbling and diving ducks in the winter months.

North of the lake is the tail section of **Ten Mile Dunes.** Among the endangered plants growing here are Mendocino coast paintbrush, Thurber's reed grass, and Menzies wallflowers. Also inhabiting this sandy world is the rare globose dune beetle. South of the dunes, an abandoned paved road gives hikers, bicyclists, and wheelchairs access to **Laguna Point Beach,** where the promontory is a good lookout for whale watching from November to March. A resident population of harbor seals haul out on the rocks just to the south. Surf fishing for rockfish, lingcod, cabezon, rock cod, and smelt is popular, as is diving for abalone.

Next stop in the state park chain is **Jug Handle State Reserve❖,** whose 769 acres straddle Route 1 five miles south of Fort Bragg. Extending from the beach at the mouth of Jug Handle Creek inland to the western boundary of Jackson State Forest, this reserve features a unique 2.5-mile nature walk known as the Ecological Staircase because it climbs through 5 terraces, each 100,000 years older and 100 feet higher than the one below it. As the Pleistocene sea level rose and fell, the land slowly rose as well, and waves cut the terraces into the sandstone cliffs. A sixth terrace is now being formed at the beach.

Each step, or terrace, on the stairway supports a different community of plants. On the first grow plants of the north coastal prairie community, including varicolored lupine and the endangered Mendocino coast paintbrush. Coast redwood dominates the second step. On the third terrace, heavy rainfall has leached nutrients from the soil, and the underlying layer of fused soil, called hardpan, can support only dwarf-sized plants. The result is a pygmy forest of fully mature Mendocino cypress and Bishop and Bolander pines that never top ten feet. The Labrador tea, rhododendron, manzanita, and huckleberry in the understory are also dwarfs. In the creek's upper watershed, sphagnum bogs nourish mosses as well as the endangered swamp harebell and sundew, an insectivorous plant that uses its sticky leaves to capture its prey.

Dotting the landscape a few miles farther south on Route 1 are a pair of small coastal parks. **Caspar Headlands State Beach and Reserve❖** features a small beach. Harbor seals frequent the offshore rocks south of the mouth of Doyle Creek, and grassy headlands along the bluff provide ideal vantage points for watching birds and whales. Nearby is **Russian Gulch State Park❖,** where a bicycle path winds

On the shore of San Francisco Bay, a male Caspian tern courts a prospective mate with an offering of food (above). The dramatic Mendocino headlands (right) rise precipitously out of an inlet of the Pacific.

through the Douglas fir and coast redwood in the lower canyon to a rocky intertidal area populated by sea urchins and abalone. A pygmy forest blankets the upper ridges on the inland side.

Surely the most photographed spot along the Mendocino coast is **Mendocino Headlands State Park❖,** a spectacular headland and marine terrace just southwest of the quaint and picturesque town that gives the county its name. Steep bluffs rising 50 to 70 feet above sea level offer vistas of rocky offshore islands, tidal pools, and an imposing sea stack just a few yards offshore. Called Goat Island, the craggy sea stack is home to more than a thousand nesting birds, including black oystercatchers, Brandt's and pelagic cormorants, and common murres. Frequent offshore winds ripple the long grasses that cover the headland. Against a backdrop of wood-framed buildings, the scene resembles a painting by Andrew Wyeth.

Just across Mendocino County's southern border is **Salt Point State Park❖,** named for the large amounts of sea salt that Kashia Pomo and Coast Yuki tribes collected from underwater crevices and used for preserving abalone, fish, and other seafood delicacies they harvested here. Designated a National Archaeological District, the park contains several midden sites, as well as the remains of a nonnative settlement. Built in the 1850s, Salt Point's Gerstle Cove featured a wooden hotel, a

blacksmith shop, and several houses.

Salt Point is also rich in natural history. Within the park's 5,000 acres are diverse habitats ranging from sandy coves to coastal hills. Investigating tidal pools along its seven miles of coastline is a popular pastime among visitors, as is diving. An active and varied sea bird colony thrives here, and Stump Beach is one of the best locations in the state to observe the breeding practices of pelagic cormorants. Black-tailed deer, gray foxes, and mountain lions are just a few of the many different types of mammals that live in the various inland plant communities, which include a pygmy forest of mature but stunted Mendocino cypress.

POINT REYES

People picturing the San Francisco Bay area are apt to conjure up images associated with urban life: the Golden Gate Bridge, colorful Fisherman's Wharf, cable cars clanging up and down steep streets, a glittering skyline, and rows of quaint Victorian houses. Yet the coastline north and south of the city limits contains some of the most spectacular wildlife in the state.

Less than an hour's drive north of the city on Route 1, **Point Reyes National Seashore**❖ is a world apart from the concrete and glass metropolis. A forest-covered ridgeline runs down the spine of a triangular peninsula bordered on the west by the gray waters of the Pacific and on the east by tranquil Tomales Bay. Within these 70,000 acres live an incredible array of wildlife. Observers have noted 438 different species of birds, dozens of types of mammals, and more than 18 percent of all the plant species found in California.

The geology and climatology of Point Reyes are responsible for its diversity. Local geologists often describe the peninsula as a great granitic whale migrating northwest. Like the gray whales that swim past California each year, the peninsula was born in the warm waters off the coast of present-day Mexico and is slowly but surely making its way toward Alaska. A geologic island, Point Reyes is connected to the North American continent only at its southeastern point. The rest has been rent from the mainland by the infamous San Andreas fault, which curves onto shore at the peninsula's southern terminus, then returns to sea at its northern tip. In geologic time, Point Reyes will soon be cleaved from the mainland altogether. Geologists estimate that it is moving northwest at about 1.29 inches per year; the rate occasionally jumps dramatically, as it did in 1906, when a major slip along the San Andreas moved the peninsula nearly 13 feet in an instant.

Scientists believe that the Point Reyes peninsula originated 225 and 140 million years ago as a collection of fine sediments deposited in a shallow lagoon some 1,700 miles south of its present location. Eventually these layers of sand, clay, and lime emerged from the sea as fine-grained rocks, and about 80 million years ago they were en-. gulfed by molten granite. Like a seagoing whale, the granitic intrusion breached and sounded, breached and sounded as it made its way north, gaining new, younger coats of sedimentary rock along the way.

At Point Reyes, these different layers of soils support so many plant communities that few other areas on the North American landmass can boast the variety of habitats found here. Within the 100-square-mile area are marine algal areas, marshland, coastal strand, northern coastal scrub, Douglas fir forest, and bishop pine forest. Among the hundreds of different plant species growing here are many endemics, including such rarities as Marin manzanita, Mount Vision ceanothus, Point Reyes bent grass, Point Reyes lupine, San Francisco owl's clover, California bottlebrush-grass, and north coast bird's-beak.

Diverse habitat combined with varied topography and temperate climate sustains an array of animals, especially birds. That combination, along with its geographic location at the western edge of the continent, makes Point Reyes a dependable refueling station for migrants as well as a hospitable wintering spot for waterfowl, passerines, and songbirds. Forty-five percent of North America's bird species have been observed here, along with many from other continents (the brown shrike, skylark, and garganey from Eurasia, to name a few).

Visitors can observe the greatest abundance of shorebirds in winter, when the tidal flats and sandy beaches bustle with black-bellied and snowy plover, long-billed curlews, dunlins, least and western sandpipers, and black oystercatchers. Seabirds are also plentiful. On the open water of Tomales Bay and Drakes Estero, look for surf scoters, greater scaup, black brant, Pacific loons, and horned grebes. Winter also offers the greatest number of raptors. Although red-tailed hawks and American kestrels are year-round residents, the colder months bring many more species, including black-shouldered kites,

Fragrant tree, or yellow bush, lupine, a deep-rooted, rapid grower, stabilizes the dunes at Point Reyes National Seashore (left). Avian residents include the tufted puffin (above), which nests on islands, and the western grebe (below), a graceful diver that engages in elaborate courtship displays.

northern harriers, ferruginous hawks, and long-eared and short-eared owls. Point Reyes is one of the few places on earth where sharp-eyed visitors can see nine different species of owl in a day.

With spring come the migrants. In February and March, flocks of tree and barn swallows gather above freshwater ponds and rivers, and in April, western flycatchers, warbling vireos, Wilson's warblers, and black-headed grosbeaks return from the tropics. In May, pelicans and Caspian terns arrive from southern breeding islands off the southern California and Mexican coasts.

Attesting that humans have long been attracted to Point Reyes too are more than a hundred Coast Miwok Indian village sites identified on the peninsula. Shellfish middens abound near Drakes Bay, named for Sir Francis Drake, who anchored here for five weeks in the summer of 1579 to repair his ship, the *Golden Hind*. Spanish explorer Don Sebastián Vizcaíno, who sought refuge from a storm in Drakes Bay on January 6, 1603, the day of the Feast of the Three Kings, named Point Reyes ("kings" in Spanish).

Today's human explorers can follow miles of trails through the park. The Bear Valley Headquarters is a good place to start because it includes a large visitor center containing interpretive exhibits. Nearby is the wheelchair-accessible Earthquake Trail, which provides a close-up view of the region's seismology and earth movements. Also nearby is a reconstructed Coast Miwok village, complete with tule structures and acorn granaries. The 4.4-mile Bear Valley Trail connects with other trails that lead hikers from the visitor center to such shoreline attractions as Sculptured Beach, named for the high cliffs that have eroded into graceful spires.

Bordering the southern tip of the seashore on both sides of Route 1 is the **Audubon Canyon Ranch–Bolinas Lagoon Preserve❖**. On the east side of the highway, 1,200 acres of sheltered water, salt marsh, and mudflat have been preserved. The lagoon is an estuary in the winter months, when freshwater runoff is high, and a saltwater lagoon in summer. The shallow water, partly due to siltation caused by past logging in the surrounding hills, is a feeding ground and nursery for 25 fish species, including starry flounders, cabezon, and several types of perch. From Route 1 visitors can see legions of plover, sandpipers, herons, and egrets feeding along the shores of Bolinas Lagoon, where extensive mudflats attract shorebirds and waterfowl by the tens of thousands. In open water, rafts of ruddy ducks, greater scaup, pintail, and surf scoters congregate.

On the inland side of the highway, four rugged canyons rise steeply from the lush coastal wetland. This rich mosaic of natural communities—forests of Douglas fir, coast redwood, and California bay mixed with grassland, coastal scrub, chaparral, and freshwater marsh—shelter numerous mammals, reptiles, amphibians, insects, and birds.

The main attraction in the canyon is the great blue herons and great egrets that nest in the tops of the tall redwood trees each spring—a noisy colony of up to 150 pairs. From a bank of telescopes at eye level across the canyon, visitors can observe the elaborate courtship of both species. Watching mates posture, display feathers, and present twigs to each other is among the biggest treats in the birding world, and after the courting, the telescopes show chicks hatching and parents rearing their young. Incubation lasts about 28 days, chick rearing 10 to 12 weeks, and both parents share the chores. Young egrets start to fly at about 7 weeks, and the heron fledglings follow 2 weeks later.

Continuing south along the Marin County coast, Route 1 passes through the 73,183-acre **Golden Gate National Recreation Area❖,** a unique collection of coastal lands administered by the National Park Service. The GGNRA, as locals fondly call it, stretches from Tomales Bay in Marin County south through San Francisco to Sweeney Ridge in San Mateo County. Although located in three highly urban counties, it encompasses surprisingly wild and open hills, canyons, and beaches, much of it former military reservation land. On the Marin side are vast expanses of open terrain; rolling hills covered with shrubs, grasses, and wildflowers; small coves, large beaches, and rocky coastal cliffs; and forested ridges and redwood valleys.

One of the most popular components of the GGNRA is **Muir Woods National Monument❖,** a 560-acre preserve of old-growth coast redwood. Just off Route 1, it features six miles of walking trails, including a self-guided nature loop through a stand of 800-year-old trees growing along Redwood Creek. With each season, the monument takes on a different look and feel. In spring, birds nest, wildflowers dot Redwood Canyon, and black-tailed deer give birth to spotted fawns in thickets of ferns. The foggy summer months are brightened by colorful azalea, aralia, and buckeye. The weather turns warm in fall, when ladybugs cluster and crayfish grow active in the creek while the forest floor acquires a red-and-yellow-splotched blanket of leaves shed by big-leaf maple trees. Come winter, the toyon berries turn red and steelhead trout and silver salmon make their annual migration up Redwood Creek to spawn. In every season, the towering redwoods stand silent and tall, a living link to the 140-million-year-old past, when their ancestors covered much of the hemisphere.

Route 1 leads south to the Golden Gate Bridge, the famous orange span over San Francisco Bay. The drowned mouth and floodplain of the Sacramento and San Joaquin rivers, San Francisco Bay has been the focus of human settlement for 4,000 years. Although much of it has become urbanized since the first Native Americans were attracted by the abundant marine life along its shores, the bay remains the state's largest single natural resource; its 460-square-mile surface provides life-sustaining habitat for many species of wildlife.

Visitors can witness the bay's bounty at **Grizzly Island State Wildlife Area❖,** which is east of Route 1 via Interstate 80 to Route 120. Southeast of Fairfield near Travis Air Force Base, this 14,300-acre complex is in the Suisun Marsh, the largest continuous estuarine marsh in the continental United States. Upward of 250,000 wintering waterfowl, thousands of shorebirds, dozens of songbird species, and seven protected species, including the endangered salt marsh harvest mouse, find refuge among the salt marshes, tidal flats, seasonal ponds, and uplands. More than 230 bird species have been counted here, including cinnamon teal, northern pintail, white pelicans, marsh wrens, common yellowthroats, golden eagles, and the elusive clapper and black rails. Several species—the Suisun aster, Suisun shrew, and Suisun sparrow—are found here and nowhere else on earth. The state's largest population of river otters live in the abundant sloughs while native tule elk graze in upland fields. From the road, visitors can watch elk rut in fall and admire the calves in spring. More than 75 miles of levee trails are open to the public.

Back on Route 1, head south through San Francisco along the San Mateo County coast to **Año Nuevo State Reserve❖** about 10 miles

---

RIGHT: *Draining from Mount Tamalpais through Muir Woods National Monument, Redwood Creek is one of the few coastal streams in the San Francisco Bay area that still supports runs of salmon and steelhead.*

south of Pescadero. Encompassing 4,000 acres of coastal bluffs, sandy beaches, dunes, and tidal pools, this reserve was established in 1958 to provide a permanent shelter for the largest mainland population of northern elephant seals in the world. It is also the biggest mainland breeding area for these lumbering giants, which visitors can view close-up. Huge bulls preside over their harems and pups along the beaches and dunes from December to March or April, making the guided walking tours (available by reservation only) one of the most popular wildlife excursions in the state.

Elephant seals are not the only attraction here. Año Nuevo also features California's biggest population of Steller sea lions, as well as a substantial breeding population of harbor seals. In addition, California thrashers, western gulls, common bushtits, cliff swallows, red-tailed hawks, California quail, and common flickers nest here.

About 25 miles south at Santa Cruz on Route 1, visitors can turn north on Route 9 and to Route 236 to **Big Basin Redwoods State Park❖.** The oldest member of the California state park system was established in 1902 when 18,000 acres were set aside to protect virgin stands of coast redwood. Big Basin, not a true basin, was formed millions of years ago by the uplifting of its circular rim and the eroding of its center by stream action. The only outlets of this bowl-like depression in the Santa Cruz Mountains are the forks of Waddell Creek, which have cut deep gorges in the rim.

The park contains more than 80 miles of hiking trails, campgrounds, historical and natural-science exhibits, waterfalls, and lush forests of coast redwood, Douglas fir, oak, and knobcone pine that are full of wildlife. Although the last grizzly bear was sighted here in the late 1800s, mountain lions, bobcats, foxes, and coyotes still stalk smaller mammals, including black-tailed deer, gray squirrels, chipmunks, opossums, and raccoon. In Big Basin's rich and diverse bird life, Steller's jays and acorn

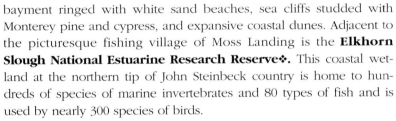

woodpeckers provide most of the noise. One of the most unusual winged inhabitants is the marbled murrelet, a web-footed shorebird the size of a robin that nests 200 feet high in the redwoods.

THE CENTRAL COAST

On its way south, Route 1 winds around Monterey Bay, a crescent-shaped embayment ringed with white sand beaches, sea cliffs studded with Monterey pine and cypress, and expansive coastal dunes. Adjacent to the picturesque fishing village of Moss Landing is the **Elkhorn Slough National Estuarine Research Reserve❖.** This coastal wetland at the northern tip of John Steinbeck country is home to hundreds of species of marine invertebrates and 80 types of fish and is used by nearly 300 species of birds.

Areas where freshwater meets salt water are some of the most productive habitats in the biological world, but they are also among the most endangered. The 900 acres on the south and east sides of Elkhorn Slough became the state's first National Estuarine Research Reserve in 1979. Another 500 acres were added later, and an adjoining 800 acres are protected by the Nature Conservancy.

The state's largest estuarine system after San Francisco Bay, Elkhorn Slough is a vital breeding and feeding ground for wildlife, including five species listed as endangered. One of the slough's rarest creatures is a shy brown bird known as the California clapper rail, which nests in the higher reaches of the salt marsh and rarely ventures far from the pickleweed. Another endangered bird is the California brown pelican, a species nearly brought to extinction by exposure to the pesticide

OVERLEAF: *Monterey cypress trees, which have the most restricted natural range of any California tree, line the Cypress Grove Trail at Point Lobos State Reserve. They also grow in nearby Pebble Beach.*

DDT. The salt ponds near the slough's mouth are the bird's most important summer roosting ground north of Point Conception. Santa Cruz long-toed salamanders inhabit several of the freshwater ponds, and the rare brackish-water snail, *Tyronia imitator*, can be found in quieter waters. The peregrine falcon haunts the slough on a seasonal basis.

The tidally bathed mudflats support a tremendous number of invertebrates. Although most of the mudflat residents are hidden from view, scientific measurements show that up to 100,000 invertebrates often live within a square meter at the surface. Elkhorn Slough, also a vital nursery and feeding area for many commercial species of fish and shellfish, flushes into the Monterey Bay submarine canyon. Deeper than the Grand Canyon, the submarine canyon is an important resource to the western Pacific fishing industry. Salmon, albacore, anchovy, rockfish, herring, and sole are just a few of the species that dwell offshore.

For millennia, the fecundity of the estuary has supported humans as well. Coastanoan Indians, also known as Ohlone, established villages by the slough 5,000 years ago, hunting tule elk and ducks and gathering shellfish. Their shell middens are still scattered along the shore, and archaeologists recently uncovered a village site at the mouth of Elkhorn Slough just 20 feet from Route 1. One of the several human skeletons found buried 10 feet below the soil surface was still wearing long strands of beads fashioned from more than 3,000 olive shells, those of a snail common in the lower slough. Bones of sea otters, harbor seals, and various seabirds were also found.

Of the five miles of trails at Elkhorn Slough Reserve, the South Marsh Loop leads from the visitor center through fields of wildflowers down to the salt marsh, which is edged with red-tipped pickleweed and other colorful succulents. Following the slough's main channel, the loop brings hikers eye to eye with dozens of species of waterfowl and shorebird.

South of Monterey and the quaint artists' colony of Carmel-by-the-Sea is **Point Lobos State Reserve❖**. Originally named Punta de los Lobos Marinos, "Point of the Sea Wolves," for the California sea lions that congregate on offshore rocks, this rocky outcropping forms the profile of a howling wolf's head when viewed from a soaring seagull's perspective. The incomparable mix of sea-lashed headlands and tree-clad beauty inspired Robert Louis Stevenson to pen *Treasure Island* after visiting here in 1879.

Point Lobos boasts a unique mosaic of bold headlands, irregular coves, and rolling meadows, a breathtaking landscape produced over millions of years by interaction between land and sea. Rocks formed below the surface were uplifted, exposed, and then shaped by waves and weather into a variety of forms. A changing sea level eroded sands and gravels from these rocks and deposited them into an array of beaches and terraces.

The reserve's soils nurture a number of plants found in only a few places in the world, including one of two native stands of Monterey cypress, one of two groves of endangered Gowen cypress, and one of four native stands of Monterey pine. To protect them, Point Lobos joined the state park system in 1933, and in 1960, 750 submerged acres were added, creating the first underwater reserve in the nation. Another 1,312 acres on the east side of Route 1 were incorporated in 1993.

Several well-marked paths wind through the reserve. One favorite, the Cypress Grove Trail, takes hikers through a stand of gnarled Monterey cypress, a hardy survivor that until the close of the Pleistocene epoch occupied a much larger range. The trail continues along the sea cliffs, providing stunning views of the rocky shoreline, endless Pacific, and passing gray, blue, and minke whales. Floating on their backs among the kelp beds below are southern sea otters, formerly found along the coast from British Columbia to Baja California. Hunted to the brink of extinction by fur trappers, they are now making a comeback under the protection of the Endangered Species Act, and Point Lobos is the heart of their sanctuary.

For the next 90 miles, Route 1 becomes unquestionably one of the most scenic highways in the world. Twisting and turning and affording spectacular views around each corner, the narrow two-lane road winds along the **Big Sur** coast. Built with convict labor in the early 1930s, Route 1 provided access to an otherwise remote and rugged stretch of land that has inspired poets and artists ever since. Because much of Big Sur was accessible only on foot or horseback before the road was completed, the area was only sparsely settled by a handful of homesteaders who built small cabins and lived off the land. Earlier, what is now Big Creek was home to two tribes of Native Americans, the Esselen and the Salinian.

Little is known about the Esselen, a small tribe numbering about a

thousand when the first Europeans arrived in 1769. Within a hundred years, Spanish padres had enticed the Esselen to move to the missions of the Salinas Valley and Monterey Peninsula, where disease and forced labor wiped them out. Anthropologists believe they were the first California native group to become extinct.

The meeting of the Pacific and the steep mountains that seem to rise from it lend Big Sur much of its beauty. As the Spanish-employed Portuguese discoverer of California, Juan Rodríquez Cabrillo, noted when sailing by in 1542, "There are mountains which seem to reach the heavens and the sea beats on them." Born of the sea, the precipitous peaks of the Santa Lucia Range are composed of thousands of feet of marine sandstone, shale, and limestone deposited along the western edge of the continent probably about 300 miles away along the southern flank of the Tehachapi Mountains in southern California. Subsequently the mountains were displaced laterally along the trace of the San Andreas fault to their present location. Much of the bedrock here has been metamorphosed, meaning that heat and pressure have changed the sandstones into quartzites, the shales into schists, and the slates and limestone into marble. The change occurred during the Age of Dinosaurs, when the area was intruded by the deep-seated granitic magmas that form the backbone of the range. Although the rocks are old, the mountains and coastline seen today are relatively youthful because the blocks forming them were uplifted only during the last 10 million years and are still rising.

Even though many believe that Big Sur deserves national-park status, the land is protected by a chain of state parks, a wilderness area, and a university reserve. The first stop heading south on Route 1 is **Garrapata State Park❖,** which features more than four miles of Big Sur coastline and an adjoining 2,879 acres of inland coastal habitat. Frequenting the coastal waters here are sea lions, harbor seals, and sea otters. The two trails connecting the coast with the rugged hills to the east pass through cactus stands and redwood groves.

Twenty-one miles south of Carmel, the Big Sur River drops steeply

---

LEFT: *Lit by the sun, pampas grasses dance in the constant winds that sweep the coast near Lucia. This section of Big Sur, where steep cliffs plunge dramatically to the Pacific, is in the Los Padres National Forest.*

LEFT: *Tolerant of many climate zones, the California quail, the black-plumed state bird, forages in large coveys and roosts low in trees and bushes.* RIGHT: *Along Route 1 near Point Sur, fields of golden wildflowers carpet the headlands above the Pacific.*

down the western face of the Santa Lucias and flattens out into a broad valley where coast redwoods, red alders, and willows grow along its banks. Steelhead and trout spawn upstream, and American dippers and two-striped garter snakes depend on the river for survival. Here **Andrew Molera State Park❖** protects 4,800 acres of meadows, woodlands, and coastline containing 10 miles of hiking and bridle trails and a walk-in campground in a wildflower-covered meadow near the beach.

Four miles farther south is **Pfeiffer Big Sur State Park❖,** 821 acres along an inland stretch of the Big Sur River. In its forests, more extensive than its northern neighbor's, sycamores, black cottonwoods, and bigleaf maples join the coast redwoods. Wild pigs and mule deer inhabit the park along with many birds, including canyon wrens, dark-eyed juncos, chestnut-backed chickadees, band-tailed pigeons, and belted kingfishers. A trail leads to Pfeiffer Falls, a beautiful waterway that dances down the rocks in a fern-lined grotto.

East of the park lie the **Los Padres National Forest** and the **Ventana Wilderness Area❖,** nearly 165,000 acres of steep-sided ridges, V-shaped valleys, and rugged terrain. Although there is little water in the wilderness area, coastal fog in the mountains at night supports dense stands of coast live oak, madrona, ponderosa pine, knobcone pine, Douglas fir, and the rare endemic Santa Lucia fir.

A meeting of mountain and sea awaits visitors about eight miles farther south on Route 1 at the **Julia Pfeiffer Burns State Park❖,** which covers 2,405 acres inland and 1,680 acres underwater. Trails lead to a redwood grove and a cypress forest atop a bluff overlooking the ocean, and also covering the hillsides are wood mint, redwood sorrel, ferns, trillium, poison oak, tanbark oak, and madrona. The animal life, which reflects the rich plant community, includes among the more unusual

reptilian species southern alligator lizards and Monterey ringneck snakes. A trail down Partington Creek leads through Partington Canyon and a 110-foot-long tunnel to the beach below, where sea otters float in a forest of kelp, feeding on sea urchins, abalone, and shellfish.

About nine miles farther south is the **Landels-Hill Big Creek Reserve❖.** Part of the University of California Natural Reserve System, this mountainous 3,858-acre preserve has been designated the California Coast Range Biosphere Reserve by UNESCO. Access is limited to special invitation or prearranged tours led by the University of California, Santa Cruz.

Nowhere else in the contiguous 48 states do mountains rise so abruptly from the ocean. Cone Peak, from which Big Creek drains, climbs 5,155 feet in a little more than 3 miles. The dramatic difference in climate between sea level and the summit creates an incredible number of spatially compressed habitat zones where 23 distinct plant communities encompass some 479 different species of vascular plants and 21 moss and liverwort species. Eight are listed by the California Native Plant Society as either rare or endangered.

Augmenting the floral diversity is Big Creek's position straddling

ABOVE: *Common coastal residents, harbor seals enjoy an enviable routine: fish dinner at high tide and then a snooze on the rocks.*
RIGHT: *As the sun sets at Pfeiffer Beach, a sea arch carved by incessant waves provides a keyhole glimpse into a magical world.*

the cool Oregon Province and the more temperate California Province. Here plants usually associated with the moist coastal forests of the north mingle with those more typical of dry southern regions, so that yucca actually grows next door to coast redwood.

Big Creek harbors many relict and endemic species as well as several disjunct ones, far from their original range. The rugged topography of the Santa Lucia Mountains has created an "island effect," and the consequent isolation has led to speciation. Santa Lucia fir and Hoover's manzanita are just two of the resulting endemics. Four species usually limited to either the Cascades or Sierra Nevada have also found their way to Big Creek: ponderosa pine, sugar pine, phantom orchid, and spotted coralroot.

The wide range of animals depending on the diverse vegetation includes 15 species of reptiles and 5 amphibians, as well as more than 125 different species of birds, among them spotted owls, goshawks, peregrine falcons, and golden eagles. The site's 51 species of mam-

mals range in size from the tiny white-footed deer mouse to the black-tailed mule deer. Bobcats are common.

A somewhat strenuous four-mile loop trail—it climbs and descends more than a thousand feet—offers a good overview of this distinctive reserve. A footbridge spans Devil's Creek above its confluence with Big Creek, which supports one of the southernmost runs of steelhead trout in the state. Together, these two streams drain nearly 24 square miles of the Santa Lucia Mountains and never run dry, even in drought years. Overhead, a canopy of coast redwood shades a natural fern grotto of Venushair, maidenhair, five-finger, sword, and bracken ferns. John Muir's favorite birds, American dippers, bob on the rocks in the middle of the creek while brown creepers cling to the sides of trees and dark-eyed juncos and hermit thrushes call from the limbs.

As the trail climbs above the creek, the redwoods are replaced by coast live oaks and other hardwoods. When the terrain turns drier, vegetation changes abruptly: Ceanothus, California coffeeberry, and coyote brush now dominate the landscape. The shrubbery opens up to a rocky overlook where three vegetation types meet: mixed hardwood forest, coastal sage scrub, and open grassland.

The different plant communities turn the natural landscape into a

ABOVE: *Purple shore crabs scuttle among tide pools along Monterey Bay's open stony shores, feeding on bits of animal matter and the algae that coat the rocks.*

beautiful mosaic. On one hillside, an open field of wild oats, blue-eyed grass, and purple needlegrass lies sandwiched between a band of ceanothus shrubs and coastal scrub. Topping it is a forest of coast live oak, madrona, and California bay. As western fence lizards sun themselves on the nearby rocks, red-tailed hawks and turkey vultures soar over the canyons, and white-throated swifts and violet-green swallows swoop low over the open faces of the hillsides. From here, visitors can see the Pacific pounding on the granite drum of the exposed rocks below.

After Big Sur, Route 1 flattens out and follows the central coast south. At the southern end of San Luis Obispo Bay, just past Pismo Beach, is an 18-square-mile area covered with sand dunes. This wind-sculpted, or "eolian," landscape is one of the few undeveloped coastal dune ecosystems in California, and the Nature Conservancy protects 4,000 acres of it as the **Guadalupe–Nipomo Dunes Preserve❖.**

These dunes are the result of several stages of dune building that began 18,000 years ago. The oldest dunes, composed of wind-borne sand carried inland from the beach and deposited in characteristic parabola-shaped mounds, are now mostly covered with plants. Closer to the beach, the younger dunes form a series of little-vegetated ridges and hollows. Still susceptible to the prevailing winds, they are more likely to be disturbed by human intrusion.

Each spring, the otherwise lunar landscape bursts into color with blooms of delicate baby blue-eyes, scarlet Indian paintbrush, and bright yellow seaside daisies. Peregrine falcons and ospreys wheel overhead as bobcats prowl hollows filled with beach grass and coyotes howl at the moon. Where the dunes meet the sea, endangered California least terns circle and western snowy plover look for food.

THE CHANNEL ISLANDS

Drivers going south on Route 1 will note that it changes to Route 101 at Las Cruces (and then back to Route 1 at Oxnard). However, visitors who want to explore the **Channel Islands National Park**❖ and **National Marine Sanctuary**❖ must leave their cars in either Santa Barbara or Ventura because the only way to reach it is by chartered boat. Five of the eight Channel Islands achieved national park status is 1980: San Miguel, Santa Rosa, Santa Cruz, Anacapa, and Santa Barbara.

ABOVE: *Tide pools hold a wealth of sea life: this vivid purple nudibranch, the elegant eolid, is also known as a Spanish shawl for its orange, fingerlike projections.*

The islands represent a unique slice of California natural history. During the last Ice Age—when sea levels were much lower, and large areas of today's seabed were dry—they were part of one vast island that geologists call Santarosae. Later, when the great continental ice sheets melted, the islands were separated.

As sea levels rose, isolating the now separate islands from the mainland, resident species developed special adaptations to cope. Others survived here while perishing on the mainland, and today 43 species and subspecies of plants are found only in the Channel Islands. Island ironwood, a member of the rose family that can grow 60 feet tall, disappeared from the mainland three million years ago, and a tiny succulent called Santa Cruz Island live-forever occupies a small patch of shoreline prairie and no other place on earth.

In adapting to island conditions, some endemic animals became larger or smaller. The most unusual is a dwarf species of mammoth that roamed Santarosae during Pleistocene times. Although the pygmy

mammoth disappeared long ago, its fossilized bones remain. Other dwarfs still survive, including the Santa Cruz gopher snake, island spotted skunk, and island fox. The latter, the smallest fox species in North America, tips the scales at barely four pounds, about one third smaller than its closest relative, the gray fox. Other species grew larger than their mainland counterparts. The Santa Cruz Island scrub jay, a subspecies endemic to this island, is 25 percent bigger and much deeper blue. The orange-crowned warbler and rufous-sided towhee have oversize body parts, especially bills and feet.

Of the Channel Islands, **Anacapa** is the closest to the mainland. Composed of three small islets accessible to one another only by boat, it features abundant marine mammals, migrating whales, and lots of birds, including western gulls, cormorants, black oystercatchers, and endangered brown pelicans. On the east island is a visitor center with a 1.5-mile self-guided nature trail designed to introduce the island.

Santa Cruz Island, managed by the Nature Conservancy, is the largest and most diverse in the chain, containing steep cliffs, gigantic sea caves, coves, sandy beaches, grassy valleys, and rugged ridge tops. Santa Cruz is especially significant because it enjoys greater biological diversity than any of the other Channel Islands—more than 625 types of plants, 217 species of birds, and 19 species of native reptiles, amphibians, and terrestrial mammals.

High mountains with deeply cut canyons, gentle rolling hills, and flat marine terraces characterize **Santa Rosa,** the second largest island. Harbor seals breed on its sandy beaches, and the eastern tip is home to a unique coastal marsh, some of the most extensive freshwater habitat on the otherwise dry chain. The island is surrounded entirely by extensive kelp forests, which foster a highly productive marine community.

San Miguel boasts outstanding natural and cultural features, including more than 500 relatively undisturbed archaeological sites, some dating back thousands of years. A seafaring Native American tribe, the Chumash, plied the Santa Barbara channel in swift canoes called tomols

LEFT: *Sea lions, migrating whales, and shipwrecks can be seen in the waters off East Anacapa, part of Channel Islands National Park.*
OVERLEAF: *On East Anacapa, winter rains produce vivid swaths of pink ice plant and yellow giant coreopsis that stretch to the horizon.*

and built villages on the larger islands. Juan Rodríguez Cabrillo, the first European to visit California, is believed to have died here.

Superb bird-watching opportunities abound on **Santa Barbara Island,** where western gulls nest in abundance along with brown pelicans. Land birds include barn owls, American kestrels, horned larks, and meadowlarks. Also living here are two threatened species: the island deer mouse and the island night lizard. A 5.5-mile self-guided nature trail provides a good overview of island life.

THE SOUTH COAST

In the southern part of the state, the California coast undergoes a dramatic change. Nearly 15 million people—more than half the state's population—live in the four counties that front the Pacific Ocean here, and another 2 million are just an hour's freeway drive inland. The appeal of the beach has made southern California coastal property among the most valuable in the world and led to a dramatic loss of habitat. Still, despite the human pressure, a few pockets of natural landscape remain.

Back on the mainland, take Route 101 to Oxnard, then head south on Route 1, passing through the **Santa Monica Mountains National Recreation Area❖** north of Los Angeles. A protected area in the making, it will eventually link 150,000 acres of city, county, and state parklands under federal management. The park provides protection for the Santa Monica Mountains, part of the Transverse Range, the only east-west–trending mountain range in coastal California and a biological island under increasing pressure from rapidly expanding Los Angeles. In its coastal salt- and freshwater marshes, tidal pools, steep canyons, and chaparral- and oak-covered mountainsides, the recreation area offers refuge to wildlife once abundant throughout southern California, such as mountain lions and golden eagles.

Visitors find plenty to do here. Hiking and riding trails lead from the beach to coastal uplands, providing stunning views of the spectacular southern California shoreline and opportunities to see deer, foxes, bobcats, hawks, and other birds. A key component of the recreation area is **Topanga State Park.** Furrowed by steep-walled canyons carved by coastal streams, it features rugged chaparral-covered ridges 2,100 feet high and scattered oak woodlands and grasslands. More than 30 miles of trails wind through it. **Upper Santa Ynez Canyon** is

ABOVE: *A rocky streambed winds through a narrow canyon in Malibu Creek State Park. Black oak, coast live oak, and manzanita populate this area of the Santa Monica Mountains National Recreation Area.*

a wildflower wonderland in spring when California poppies, wild mustard, and other blooming plants put on their colorful display.

Wedged between housing subdivisions off Route 1 in Orange County is the **Upper Newport Bay Ecological Reserve❖,** a remnant riverbed carved during the Pleistocene that contains hundreds of acres of productive wetlands. The mudflats conceal littleneck clams, polychaete worms, and other invertebrates prized by thousands of shorebirds, including various species of plover and sandpipers. Ospreys, egrets, brown pelicans, and mergansers feed on anchovies and California killifish in the bay's shallow waters. On the tiny islands that dot the bay are nesting American avocets, California least terns, and black-necked stilts. The clapping sound heard near the thickets of cordgrass that line the shore is the unique call of the endangered light-footed clapper rail. A cousin, the threatened black rail, also lives here. In the coastal sage scrub above the bay lives another threatened bird, the California gnatcatcher, whose mewing call sounds like a kitten's meow.

In San Clemente, Route 1 is swallowed up by Interstate 5, which hugs

the coast south to the Mexican border. Just past the coastal town of Del Mar is **Los Peñasquitos Lagoon–Torrey Pines State Reserve❖.** The lagoon is a 600-acre wetland consisting of coastal salt marsh with deep tidal channels and pocket areas of mudflats and salt flats. Pickleweed, salt grass, and sea lavender dominate the salt marsh plant community while cattails and bulrushes grow in the shallow brackish waters, providing nesting sites for several endangered bird species, including the California least tern, Belding's savannah sparrow, and light-footed clapper rail. Green-backed herons, snowy egrets, willet, dowitchers, and other migratory shorebirds are present in fall and spring.

ABOVE: *Only a few inches long, the spiky coast horned lizard inflates when frightened, making it an unruly mouthful.*
LEFT: *In Del Mar, a rare Torrey pine and large golden-flowered agaves grow along a trail in the Torrey Pines State Reserve.*

Adjoining the lagoon to the south is a thousand-acre coastal bluff reserve that is home to one of the world's rarest pine trees, the Torrey pine. Some of the best examples of this wind-tortured tree grow in the North Grove area, traversed by a .6-mile self-guided nature trail that affords panoramic views of the coast from the top of rugged sandstone cliffs. At the beginning of Perry Grove trail is the **Whitaker Memorial Native Plant Garden,** named for the botanist who discovered the Torrey pine. Along this and other trails from the reserve's visitor center, watch for abundant wildlife, including California quail, scrub jays, gray foxes, southern mule deer, bobcats, and brush rabbits. The hillside chaparral is home to California thrashers, ravens, and loggerhead shrikes, and soaring above the bluffs are great horned owls and American kestrels.

The final and most southerly natural area on the California coast is the **Tijuana River National Estuarine Research Reserve❖,** some 2,531 acres of tidally flushed wetland, riparian, and upland habitats along the nation's border with Mexico. The estuary is bathed twice a day by seawater moving over the salt marsh, and twice a day the wetlands are exposed to intensive sunlight and drying winds.

169

This intermingling of water and soil, marine and terrestrial influences creates a nurturing habitat for wildlife. In the mudflats reside the most diverse species in the world: invertebrates. Worms, clams, horn snails, and crabs live here in abundance, attracting thousands of hungry shorebirds. Of the 27 species that feed in the estuary's mudflats, willet, dowitchers, sandpipers, and marbled godwits are the most numerous.

Because of its location on the Pacific Flyway, the estuary is also a wintering site for many birds. More than 371 species have been sighted here, including red-throated loons, double-crested cormorants, red-breasted mergansers, and elegant terns. Among the species nesting here are pied-billed grebes, snowy egrets, northern pintail, black-necked stilts, and American avocets. Tijuana Slough is a bastion for six endangered species too: Belding's savannah sparrows, California least terns, light-footed clapper rails, least Bell's vireos, peregrine falcons, western brown pelicans, and the threatened snowy plover.

A network of trails loops through the reserve. One trail circles an extensive tidal pond and leads to the banks of the Tijuana River. A stretch of dunes on the western edge acts as a coastal barrier, preventing the ocean from inundating the marsh. A windblown, salty, and arid environment, the dunes are spotted with ambrosia, beach evening primroses, and sea rocket, and the surface runners of sand verbena and dune morning glory help stabilize the shifting sand.

In estuaries, the ocean's nurseries, more than two thirds of the nation's commercially important fish and shellfish spawn, nurse, or feed. In Tijuana Slough, topsmelt, northern anchovies, opaleye, and white croakers breed and give birth in small tidal creeks and channels covered with the bright green algae called sea lettuce.

The uplands above the salt marsh sustain aromatic sagebrush, flat-topped buckwheat, jaumea, and alkali heath, collectively known as coastal sage scrub, which once covered much of southern California. Today, after decades of human development, coastal scrub is one of the most endangered plant communities in the state, a vivid reminder of just how fragile natural California is.

RIGHT: *Eroded sandstone badlands as rippled as the waves offshore— remnants of dunes and barrier beaches that were formed 20 million years ago—complement the sunset at Torrey Pines State Reserve.*

NEVADA

PART TWO

N E V A D A

J ust as California deserves its golden sobriquet, Nevada merits its reputation as the Silver State—and not simply because of the ore that lured prospectors here in 1859. Scene after natural scene reflects the shine of the metal—from the silica and mica that glisten in the endless sand dunes of the Big Smoky Valley to the glacier-scoured peaks and canyons of the Ruby Mountains, from the clumps of big sagebrush that cover the Alvord Desert to the shimmering waters of the seasonal playa lakes that come and go in the blink of an eye.

Although Nevada is most famous for the desert gambling mecca of Las Vegas, game not gaming, habitats not hotels are its greatest natural attractions. Despite being the driest of all 50 states, Nevada is among the top 10 in natural diversity. It boasts the biggest cutthroat trout ever caught, seven kinds of rattlesnake, the largest herd of horses still galloping wild and free, rivers that flow in not out, more mountain ranges than any other state, and temperatures that fluctuate 160 degrees.

Nevada is a vast, lonely country divided between two deserts. The Mojave spills over from California, rendering the southern tip of the state so hot and dry that creosote bush, Joshua trees, and Mojave yucca dominate the plant life. The northern three quarters of the state falls within the Great Basin, a triangular biogeographic province that stretches to the crest of the Sierra Nevada in the west, the Rocky Mountains and Colorado River drainage in the east, and the Snake River country in the north. Cooler and wetter, the Great Basin spans the breadth of Nevada in a series of basins and ranges

PRECEDING PAGES: *In Fire Canyon rippled clouds highlighted against a brilliant blue desert sky mimic the overlapping folds and contrasting colors of the sandstone below in Nevada's Valley of Fire State Park.*

patterned like the folds of an accordion.

Nevada is a sparsely populated, strangely beautiful, subtly dynamic land, perhaps best described in *Mormon Country* by the late novelist and essayist Wallace Stegner, a Great Basin native son:

> Three or four little puddles, an interminable string of crazy, warped, arid mountains with broad valleys swung between them; a few waterholes, a few springs . . . a few little valleys where irrigation is possible and where the alfalfa looks incredibly green as you break down out of the pass . . . that about sums up the Great Basin. Its rivers run nowhere but into the ground; its lakes are probably salty or brackish; its rainfall is negligible and its scenery depressing to all but the few who have lived in it long enough to acquire a new set of values about scenery. Its snake population is large and its human population small. Its climate shows extremes of temperature that would tire out anything but a very strong thermometer. It is a dead land, though a very rich one.

Rich indeed. Nevada is rich not only in geologic marvels—150 mountain ranges, 31 peaks above 11,000 feet, vast playas, huge Pleistocene lakes, lush riparian corridors, and brutal desert—but in wildlife as well. Living in the state's 70 million acres and along its 2,760 miles of rivers and streams are 370 species of birds, 129 mammals, 64 reptiles and amphibians, and 46 fish. The creosote-bush scrubland is home to dozens of cactus species along with desert tortoises, desert bighorn, kangaroo rats, and bobcats. In the low and well-watered areas, western kingbirds, song sparrows, yellow warblers, and marsh wrens nest among alders, water birches, and willows. Oceans of sagebrush support black-tailed jackrabbits, mule deer, pronghorn, prairie falcons, and golden eagles. Rising from them are "island" mountains, where Rocky Mountain elk, golden-mantled ground squirrels, and Clark's nutcrackers live in and above forests of pinyon-juniper, mountain mahogany, and limber and bristlecone pine.

Although many of Nevada's wildlife species can be found in other states within the provinces of the Great Basin and Mojave deserts, some are unique. Nevada ranks among the top ten states for total number of globally rare species. Just west of Las Vegas, for instance, are two areas that between them harbor nearly 70 endemic species—those that live naturally nowhere else. The Spring Mountains rise nearly 12,000 feet and support 35 endemic plants, 8 butterflies, and the state's only endemic mammal, Palmer's chipmunk. Nearby Ash Meadows provides a refuge for the Devil's Hole pupfish and two dozen other endemics.

Isolation and a complex geologic genealogy have created this El Dorado of endemism. Half a billion years ago Nevada was covered by water, a shallow shelf of seafloor slanting toward a deep ocean trench. Over time this seafloor rose and fell, and the covering seas came and went. Off the western edge of the shelf continental plates smashed into each other, pushing mountains violently skyward and causing huge blocks of rock to tilt or collapse—an ongoing process as evidenced by Nevada's active faults and young volcanic rocks. Weather also went to work, bringing alternating periods of icy cold and moist warmth. The result is a myriad of soils and a multitude of elevations continuously being separated from one another by restless geologic forces and an ever-changing climate—factors conducive to nurturing distinctive plants and animals and fostering their evolutionary differences.

Along with endemism, however, come the hazards of rarity and endangerment. Of Nevada's animal species, 30 are federally listed as endangered. Another 110 are candidates for listing. Although only 8 plant species have been so named, 203 more are being considered. Nevada holds the dubious distinction of having more species of fish listed as endangered, threatened, or of special concern than any other state in the union—43 to be exact. Since 1940, eight more have gone the way of the dodo—and those are only the documented examples. No doubt others have also passed into oblivion.

Pressures exerted on the land by Nevada's phenomenal

OVERLEAF: *Like islands marooned in a vast sagebrush ocean, the rolling Pancake Range rises in central Nevada near Warm Springs. A rare rainstorm waters clumps of yellow rabbitbrush that dot the terrain.*

NEVADA

50   0   50 Miles

50   0   50 Kilometers

ABOVE: *Sphinxlike sandstone monoliths, part of a vast sandy desert millions of years ago, were weathered by wind and time creating a natural outdoor sculpture garden at Valley of Fire State Park.*

growth are partly responsible for such a high rate of extinction and endangerment. Its population of approximately 1.5 million, up nearly 39 percent since 1980, has multiplied faster than any other state's. Most of the increase has occurred in Nevada's two metropolitan areas, spurred by the burgeoning gambling and entertainment industry. Las Vegas is the fastest-growing city in the country, up a whopping 350 percent since 1980. In the early 1990s alone, Las Vegas was adding 322 new residents every day, many seeking jobs created by the billions spent on constructing new resort hotels. The Reno metropolitan area is also exploding, doubling in population in just 20 years.

Such massive population growth has had a tremendous impact on the environment, especially in the Las Vegas and Washoe valleys.

ABOVE: *Near a watering hole in the Red Desert, two stallions compete for mares. Herds of wild mustangs, the legacy of Spaniards and generations of cowboys, still roam Nevada's wide-open basins.*

Air quality has deteriorated significantly because of an increase in cars and trucks. The ever-fragile water supply in this driest of all states has become even more imperiled. And raw land is being converted to residential, commercial, and industrial use at a furious rate.

Other blows to Nevada's natural ecosystem have resulted from a recent mining boom. Now the world's fourth-largest producer of gold, Nevada contains more than 600,000 claims; 350,000 of those are active, and 150 open pits are presently in production. Mining operations destroy habitat, produce toxins, and promote population increase and development. The town of Elko, for instance, has grown 50 percent since 1986 because of a surge in the mining industry.

Overgrazing is also a problem. Nevada has a higher propor-

ABOVE: *After the winter rains, white-flowered birdcage evening primrose and pink desert sand verbena carpet the landscape near Lake Mead.*
RIGHT: *At dusk white-tailed deer graze in one of the many broad valleys that alternate with high, craggy mountains in Great Basin National Park.*

tion—nearly 87 percent—of public lands than any other state except Alaska. Of the more than 700 grazing allotments on the 48 million acres administered by the Bureau of Land Management (BLM), all but 4 percent are now in less-than-ideal condition as a result of overgrazing. The practice has been linked to widespread habitat destruction, which endangers many wildlife species, including the threatened desert tortoise.

Despite such encroachments, Nevada remains largely open and undeveloped. Although it boasts only one national park, it contains 7.4 million acres of national forest with 38 major recreational sites, 8 national wildlife refuges, 14 officially designated wilderness areas, 22 state parks, 11 local or county parks, 9 BLM recreational areas, and a national recreation area. In all these places, visitors can still find natural Nevada.

This book divides the state into two different regions. Chapter 5 explores southern Nevada, and Chapter 6 moves on to the distinctive basin-and-range topography of northern Nevada.

Nevada's land is large and lonely but oh-so-beautiful. "Remember," wrote novelist and critic Bernard De Voto in *The Year of Decision*, "that the yield of a hard country is a love deeper than a fat and easy land inspires, that throughout the arid west the Americans have found a secret treasure . . . a stern and desolate country, a high bare country, a country brimming with a beauty not to be found elsewhere."

He was right.

SOUTHERN NEVADA

To a visitor standing on the fabled Las Vegas Strip beneath a summer sun surrounded by neon-pulsing coin-ringing air-conditioned gambling halls, the city resembles a modern-day wagon train pulled into a circle to guard against the elements. A view in any direction from the top of a high-rise hotel confirms that impression. Vegetation on the remaining undeveloped land is sparse. Pockets of alkali shimmer in the glare of cloudless skies. Heat-induced mirages float just out of reach. And the sound of water running over rocks is simply an illusion created inside some of the newer casinos–cum–theme parks.

Sun, sky, and sand embrace Las Vegas in an unrelenting grip. Humans were never meant to live in such an extreme climate in the numbers found in Las Vegas, where temperatures range from 8 degrees in January to 116 Fahrenheit in July and a year's rainfall would barely fill a coffee cup. It's too dry to farm, too harsh to remain outside very long. Without the dream of a gangster named Bugsy Siegel, water piped in from the Colorado River, and cheap electricity from Hoover Dam, Las Vegas would be just like all the other towns sprinkled across the Mojave Desert—small and isolated.

Although glittering Las Vegas may be the porch light that draws most

LEFT: *Like some gigantic petrified mastodon, Elephant Rock with its distinctive "trunk" is just one of many eroded red sandstone formations that provoke the imagination at Valley of Fire State Park.*

people to southern Nevada, it is not all there is to see. Centered in some of the most inhospitable terrain on earth, but also surrounded by some of the most biologically diverse, the region is sure to surprise.

Nevada encompasses two deserts, the Mojave and the Great Basin. Biogeographers trace the oscillating boundary about a hundred miles north of Las Vegas, roughly between the border towns of Dyer at the California line and Uvada at the Utah line. The more southern Mojave is hotter and drier, distinguished by creosote bush, Joshua trees, and Mojave yucca; the cooler, wetter Great Basin is marked by pinyon-juniper and sagebrush. The dividing line is really a transition zone, where Joshua trees slip across the border in one direction and sagebrush in the other.

Superb examples of the Mojave Desert ecosystem can be found within earshot of Las Vegas's slots. In natural areas such as the Desert National Wildlife Range, Ash Meadows National Wildlife Refuge, and Lake Mead National Recreation Area exists a complex web of life whose gossamerlike threads are all the more astonishing in the harsh conditions they face. Although these areas share traits common throughout the sprawling Mojave, each is distinctive. Climate, geology, and even the hand of man have conspired to create unique worlds within the larger desert universe. Ash Meadows, for instance, boasts 26 species found naturally nowhere else on the planet. Isolation also plays a role in shaping the region's biodiversity. In the nearby Spring Mountains, at least another 30 different endemic species can be found.

Biology does not monopolize uniqueness in this corner of the state, either. Southern Nevada is brimming with a fantastic assortment of geologic wonders. No more than fifteen minutes from the fabled Las Vegas Strip in one direction and an hour in the other lie two stretches of pavement lined with neon-colored skyscrapers. No concrete, glass, or fluorescent tubes were used to create these beauties, however. The towering sandstone escarpments at Red Rock Canyon National Conservation Area and Valley of Fire State Park are the work of hundreds of millions of years of earth, wind, and fire.

OVERLEAF: *In central Nevada, the empty road goes on forever across wide basins and high ranges, earning Route 50 its sobriquet, "The Loneliest Highway." This stretch is near Great Basin National Park.*

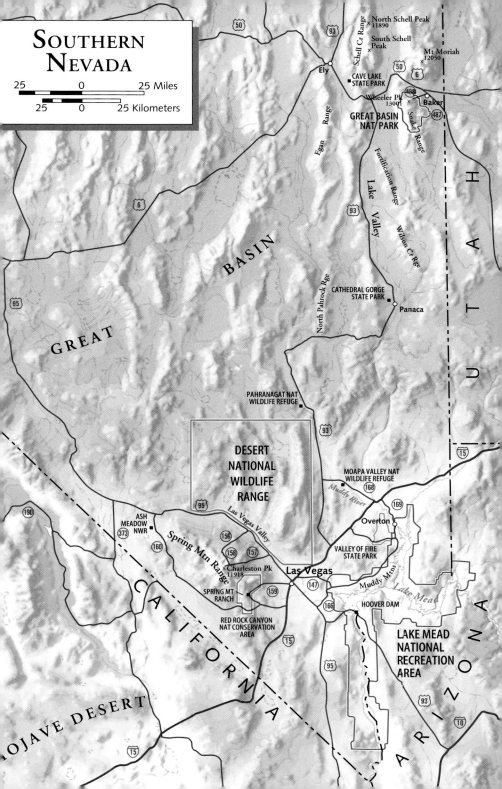

SOUTHERN NEVADA

25   0   25 Miles
25   0   25 Kilometers

GREAT BASIN

GREAT

50

93

Schell Cr Range

North Schell Peak
x 11890

South Schell
Peak
x

Mt Moriah
x 12050

Ely

50

6

CAVE LAKE
STATE PARK

Wheeler Pk
13001   x

488

Baker

487

**GREAT BASIN
NAT PARK**

Snake Range

Egan   Range

Fortification Range

Lake   Valley

Wilson Cr Rge

93

6

95

North Pahroc Rge

CATHEDRAL GORGE
STATE PARK

Panaca

U T A H

PAHRANAGAT NAT
WILDLIFE REFUGE

93

15

**DESERT
NATIONAL
WILDLIFE
RANGE**

MOAPA VALLEY NAT
WILDLIFE REFUGE

168

Muddy River

169

190

ASH
MEADOW
NWR

373

95

Las Vegas Valley

Overton

Spring Mtn Range

156

158   157

Charleston Pk
11918

**VALLEY OF FIRE
STATE PARK**

160

Las Vegas

147

**SPRING MT
RANCH**

159

Muddy Mtns

166

HOOVER DAM

Lake Mead

**RED ROCK CANYON
NAT CONSERVATION
AREA**

15

95

**LAKE MEAD
NATIONAL
RECREATION
AREA**

C A L I F O R N I A

A R I Z O N A

MOJAVE DESERT

15

10

Northeast of Las Vegas the land changes from Mojave to Great Basin. Snowcapped mountains rise from oceans of sagebrush. Desert turns to alpine in just a couple of miles —miles that go straight up. The showcase of this area is Great Basin National Park, one of America's newest and Nevada's only. A park road that climbs 10,000 feet to the top elevates the soul as well as the body. The view from the summit gives a perspective on the state that no high-rise hotel window can match.

This exploration of the natural areas surrounding Las Vegas begins northwest of town with the dramatic cliffs of Red Rock Canyon, the two endemic strongholds of Ash Meadows and the Spring Mountains, and the sprawling Desert National Wildlife Range. It then proceeds east to nearby Lake Mead National Recreation Area and adjoining Valley of Fire State Park. From there, the route continues northeast, encountering the small but surprising Moapa Valley and Pahranagat national wildlife refuges, the inspiring bentonite cliffs of Cathedral Gorge, and finally the splendor of the nation's newest national park, Great Basin.

ABOVE: *The flowers of these desert four o'clocks actually don't open until evening. Native Americans chewed the large root and ground it into powder for poultices.*

RIGHT: *Seemingly oblivious to their spectacular surroundings, wild burros greet visitors to Red Rock Canyon from their grazing grounds alongside scenic Route 159.*

NORTHWEST OF LAS VEGAS

Visitors needn't drive far to discover a world very different from the climate- and sensory-controlled atmosphere of downtown Las Vegas. From the Strip, head west on Route 159 (Charleston Boulevard) 15 miles to **Red Rock Canyon National Conservation Area❖.** This 195,610-acre geologic gemstone, supervised by the Bureau of Land Management, features a 13-mile scenic drive through multicolored sandstone escarpments and a lush valley that was home to teeming forests and marine creatures in Jurassic times. Although the dinosaurs

have disappeared, the site still sustains numerous species of wildlife.

Hollywood film crews frequently use Red Rock Canyon as a cinematic backdrop because few sites can match its breathtaking scenery. Here, as a result of powerful geologic forces, cliffs the color of Georgia O'Keeffe paintings rise dramatically 2,000 feet above the valley floor. Two hundred million years ago, Nevada was a floor of gray limestone lying beneath a warm, shallow sea. As the sea retreated, sand dunes spread across the land (the color comes from leached red iron oxide). About 95 million years ago, two of the earth's crustal plates collided with such force that whole sections of buried gray limestone were thrust up and over the younger sandstone. (Today's red color comes from red iron oxide leached after the sandstone was deposited.) Since then, wind and rain have carved steep-walled canyons and fashioned uniformly contoured boulders.

Begin at the world-class visitor center for an overview of the region's intriguing natural history. It offers films, dioramas, and literature on resident plant and animal life, as well as insights into the region's remarkable geology. Afterward, follow the one-way scenic loop drive taking time to explore the more than 20 miles of hiking trails. The first stop is the Calico Hills, capped by 6,323-foot **Turtle Head Peak.** Two overlooks feature colorful sandstone formations and exposed crossbedded sandstone, which resembles a cross-section of a cappuccino. Any number of short paths lead down to bedrock.

Next, an easy walk of a hundred yards takes visitors to the historic turn-of-the-century sandstone quarry. Trailheads to excellent hiking and rock-climbing areas are well marked. Willow Spring is a favorite area for nature photographers, and Lost Creek Canyon provides access to some of the area's prolific plant, bird, and animal life. Watch for the bighorn sheep that are plentiful here. Ice Box Canyon, named for the sheets of icicles that form on the north-facing wall during midwinter freezes, is popular among rock climbers, who must don crampons and ice axes during cold snaps. The hiking trail through Pine Creek Canyon leads to lush riparian zones and a remnant stand of

---

LEFT: *Ash trees turn gold and crimson along Oak Creek Canyon in the Red Rock Canyon National Conservation Area. Because of the magnificent scenery, these canyons have appeared in many western movies.*

ABOVE: *Pinyon pine and manzanita grow over a montane chaparral in the rugged Spring Mountains, home to 20 species of endemic flowering plants and 8 species of native invertebrates found nowhere else.*

ponderosa pine, growing here at its lowest elevation in the state. In fall the canyon brims with vibrant colors.

At the foot of the canyon are the sheer buff-colored Wilson Cliffs, and nestled at the base is **Spring Mountain Ranch❖.** This 528-acre state park was established as a cattle ranch in 1869. Its cool temperatures, plentiful water, and lush grassy meadows still attract the wild burros that graze alongside the road and the numerous songbirds that perch on the cottonwoods and willows lining the creek. The New England–style red ranch house complete with white picket fence serves as a visitor center and provides self-guiding tour brochures. The park is a popular spot for picnickers, and sunsets here are reputedly among the best in the state.

Route 159 dead-ends into Route 160, which leads 75 miles northwest to **Ash Meadows National Wildlife Refuge❖.** Established in

ABOVE: *Known by many names, including panther, puma, and cougar, the mountain lion, a silent, solitary hunter, stalks deer and smaller mammals in the wild, semiarid terrain of the Spring Mountains.*

1984, this 23,447-acre oasis provides habitat for at least 24 plants and animals found nowhere else in the world. Four endemic fish swimming in its spring-fed wetlands—three desert pupfish and one speckled dace—are presently on the endangered species list. The most famous, the Devil's Hole pupfish, lives near the surface of a 55-by-10-foot limestone pool, one of the most restricted habitats of any known vertebrate. Ash Meadows enjoys a greater concentration of endemic species than any other local area in the United States and the second-largest on the entire continent.

One of the last desert oases in the southwestern part of the country, the refuge is a major discharge point for a vast underground water system stretching a hundred miles to the northeast. All the water is "fossil" water, meaning that it entered the groundwater system thousands of years ago. It comes to the surface at more than 30 seeps and springs at

195

Ash Meadows, providing a rich and complex variety of habitats.

The history of Ash Meadows' unusual concentration of unique species began 12,000 years ago, at the end of the Pleistocene era, when the cool, wet climate left the region covered by large interconnected lakes and rivers. As the climate grew warmer, causing these lakes to recede, various species were separated and isolated. The earliest known human inhabitants were Paiute Indians attracted by the area's abundant freshwater and wildlife. During the 1960s much of Ash Meadows was developed for agricultural use. In 1984 the Nature Conservancy recognized the need to protect the unique habitat and acquired more than 12,000 acres, eventually turning them over to the U.S. Fish and Wildlife Service for management.

Although restoration and improvement efforts are still under way—the plan specifies expanding the refuge and managing the entire area as a natural ecosystem—visitors can explore Ash Meadows by hiking its limited trails. The refuge offers excellent opportunities to view its abundant birdlife because it is a prime winter stopover for thousands of ducks and geese. Waterfowl include great blue herons, eared grebes, snowy egrets, sandpipers, white-faced ibis, American avocets, and black-necked stilts. Verdins, crissal thrashers, Bewick's wrens, phainopeplas, loggerhead shrikes, and blue grosbeaks can often be spotted in the upland areas.

Plant life at Ash Meadows is nothing short of amazing considering its location in the seemingly inhospitable Mojave Desert. Among the threatened and endangered species of flora are Ash Meadows blazing star, Ash Meadows sunray, Ash Meadows milk vetch, Amargosa niterwort, spring-loving centaury, and Ash Meadows ivesia. Although alkali mariposa lily and Tecopa bird's beak are listed only as sensitive species, many botanists believe they qualify for threatened or endangered status.

From Ash Meadows, take Route 95 south toward Las Vegas, turning west on Route 156 into Lee Canyon for a spectacular drive through the **Toiyabe National Forest** and the beautiful **Spring Mountain National Recreation Area❖.** Even more endemic species can be found here, although they are spread over a much greater area than the more localized concentration found at Ash Meadows.

Capped by 11,918-foot **Charleston Peak,** the Spring Mountains form the western wall of Las Vegas Valley. Tall and rugged and often snowcapped, the mountains are a forested island poking out of a sea of sand. Their elevation—five life zones ranging from Mojave Desert to alpine—and climate—typically 20 to 30 degrees cooler and 25 inches wetter than Las Vegas, just 45 minutes away—have isolated the flora growing here. As a result, approximately 18 species of endemic flowering plants live within the 50-mile-long range, most of them in the upper reaches. These include several species of penstemon, milk vetch, and angelica. Among the most eye-catching are endemic chain ferns that grow to six feet and rough angelica, whose white flower clusters on stems two or more feet tall resemble Queen Anne's lace. The rarest of the alpine species is the arching pussytoes, a dwarf member of the aster family.

Endemic animal life in the Spring Mountains, also prolific, encompasses eight species of invertebrates—butterflies and an ant—and a chipmunk. In addition, deer, bobcats, mountain lions, and a variety of bird species, including raptors, live in the canyons and along the ridges. The mountains provide crucial summer habitat for a sizable herd of desert bighorn sheep.

Despite its proximity to Las Vegas, most of the Spring Mountain Range is wilderness, by natural definition if not by official designation (one large chunk around Charleston Peak has already been designated, and three more areas are under consideration for federal protection). The best way to get around these parts is on foot. The Forest Service maintains several good trails in the central part of the range, including a 17-mile loop around Charleston Peak that leads through forests of ponderosa pine, white fir, bristlecone pine, and mountain mahogany shading thickets of elderberry, and aspen brush. In July showy orange paintbrush, red columbine, shooting stars, and blue penstemons add color to the trail. Near the top, where breathtaking views overlook steep cliffs, the forest gives way to bristlecone pine.

Route 156 forms a loop with Route 157, which leads out of the Spring Mountains via Kyle Canyon. Back on Route 95, cross over to the **Desert National Wildlife Range❖.** At 1.5 million acres (more than 2,200 square miles), it is the largest wildlife refuge in the contiguous United States (although a large portion is part of the Nellis Air Force Base Test Range and therefore off-limits to the public). Established primarily to protect desert bighorn sheep, it also provides refuge for mule

ABOVE: *Created in 1935 when the Hoover Dam was opened to tame the Colorado River below the Grand Canyon, Lake Mead today presents a*

deer, coyotes, badgers, bobcats, foxes, and mountain lions. More than 260 bird species have been identified here, including phainopepla, roadrunner, pinyon jay, red-tailed hawk, and golden eagle.

An auto route leads through the heart of the refuge, crossing three plant communities: desert shrub, desert woodland, and coniferous forest. Creosote bush and white bur sage dominate the hotter, lower elevations, yielding to Mojave yucca and cactus 2,000 feet above the valley floor. From the 4,000 to 6,000-foot range, Joshua trees and blackbrush take over. Desert bighorn sheep often inhabit these elevations, as do loggerhead shrikes, cactus wrens, and sage sparrows. Above 6,000 feet Joshua trees become scarce and are replaced by pinyon pines and Utah junipers. Big sagebrush dots the ground. Desert bighorn and mule deer can be spotted near springs, as can broad-tailed hummingbirds and common bushtits. From 7,000 to 9,000 feet ponderosa pines and white firs grow. In their branches Clark's nutcrackers and white-breasted nuthatches produce a sound quite different from the jangle of slot machines just 30 miles away.

198

singular landscape of desert, lake, and rock. The vast national recreation area is now home to anglers and sailors, palm trees and sunsets.

WATER AND FIRE: EAST AND NORTH OF LAS VEGAS

Earth, wind, and fire all shape the lands east of Las Vegas. From Route 147 (Lake Mead Boulevard) turn north on Route 167 (Northshore Scenic Drive), where the senses are jarred by the sudden appearance of a great body of water that fills the surrounding canyons and laps at the base of mountains as far as the eye can see. **Lake Mead National Recreation Area❖** was created in 1936 with the completion of 726-foot-high **Hoover Dam,** a concrete colossus that backed up the Colorado River from Black Canyon 110 miles east to Grand Canyon National Park in Arizona. The area grew again in 1953 with the completion of the Davis Dam and the creation of Lake Mojave.

Twice the size of Rhode Island, this huge area features a very unnatural lake in a most natural setting. Although the 162,700-acre reser-

---

OVERLEAF: *Annual winter rains transform the arid, brown desert hills encircling Lake Mead, producing such brilliantly colored spring wildflowers as yellow poppies, purple phacelia, and white blazing stars.*

voir caters primarily to boaters and anglers, the recreation area provides access to an expanse of desert wilderness. Despite all the water,
the desert reigns supreme here. Less than four inches of rain falls a
year, making it one of the driest places on the planet. Summer temperatures can reach 120 degrees Fahrenheit.

The land is a rugged mix of towering mountains, stark plateaus,
windswept desert basins, vertical-walled canyons, and winding desert
washes. Vegetation is generally limited to creosote bush, Mormon tea,
and cactus, which dot the otherwise empty landscape like stubbles on
a chin. Other plants are easily missed except after winter rains, when
they spring to life for short periods of time, spraying bursts of color
against a mountain backdrop of browns, blacks, reds, and grays.

The desert surrounding Lake Mead is far from lifeless, however.
For the patient, ample wildlife is on view. Inhabiting the recreation
area are more than a thousand desert bighorn sheep, one of the few
desert animals active in the extreme heat of the day. During the cooler
hours look for rock, antelope, and round-tailed ground squirrels;
black-tailed jackrabbits; spotted and striped skunks; kit and gray
foxes; coyotes; and various kinds of mice and rats. Reptiles are plentiful, including desert tortoises, desert iguanas, chuckwallas, Gila mon-

Although called a California king snake, the long-lived constrictor is found throughout Nevada. The dark snake displays various patterns including white bands (left) and stripes (right). Western diamondback rattlesnakes (above) buzz a warning before striking.

sters, banded geckos, horned lizards, long-nosed snakes, western diamondback rattlesnakes, and common king snakes. Birds are plentiful too. In the upland areas, greater roadrunners, lesser nighthawks, western meadowlarks, quail, doves, and numerous kinds of wrens, warblers, and flycatchers catch the eye. Along the water are abundant western grebes, great blue herons, Canada geese, mallard, western sandpipers, avocets, California gulls, and double-crested cormorants.

While driving along the lake's northern shore on Route 167, stop at the **Redstone Picnic Area❖.** This colorful formation of red stone dunes was once part of a vast sea of sand dunes created when dinosaurs roamed the earth (a 30-minute hike loops around the closest formation). In a climate hotter and drier than today's, strong winds throughout the Southwest piled up sand in great dunes that eventually hardened into a formation called Aztec sandstone. Groundwater leaching and oxidizing iron deposits colors the jumble of rocks various shades of orange, red, purple, tan, and white. Look closely at the pockmarked face of the formations: More often than not the holes house lizards, turning the cliffs into reptilian high-rise apartments.

An even greater display of honeycombed Aztec sandstone overlooks the shores of Lake Mead at the aptly named **Valley of Fire State Park❖,**

off Route 169 near the town of Overton. Here, 36,000 acres reveal millions of years of geology in a stunning display of brightly colored pinnacles, arches, columns, cliffs, gullies, and canyons.

The rocks underlying the Valley of Fire are much older—probably dating back 1.7 billion years—but the ones that can be readily seen were created when the region was a vast sea. Hundreds of feet deep and extending from horizon to horizon, its warm waters nurtured simple plants and animals. Over the next 300 million years these ocean-living life-forms evolved into a profusion of complex creatures that filled nearly every possible niche, and layer upon layer of lime mud and shells discarded from sea creatures were deposited one on another like the layers of a cake.

About 200 million years ago the seafloor slowly rose as the Pacific plate moved against the North American plate, lifting the land near the Valley of Fire even higher. In time the sea receded completely, leaving a layer of gray limestone mud measuring several miles thick. As various deposits of sand and gravel were laid down, exposure to the air caused the iron and metal compounds in these sediments to oxidize and form rust. The result is a brilliant

LEFT: *A rippling landscape of red Mesozoic sandstone formations stretches to meet the Muddy Mountains, gray limestone peaks from the earlier Paleozoic era, which surround the Valley of Fire.*

collection of reds, pinks, purples, and lavenders.

Like much of the Southwest, the Valley of Fire was covered by a great sandy desert 140 million years ago, after the region's climate changed. Huge dunes thousands of feet tall towered over the landscape. These dunes eventually fossilized, and the resulting sandstone was etched by wind and fractured by faults. Over time the continual movement of the earth's crustal plates added new shapes to the landscape by pushing the gray limestone beds of the Paleozoic sea up through the sandstone, creating a range of tall and rugged peaks that abut the park to the southwest, the **Muddy Mountains.**

To enjoy the beauty of Nevada's oldest state park and experience its wonder, begin at the visitor center, where dioramas and photographic exhibits explain the region's remarkable geologic history. There is a good selection of literature on the subject, and staff are on hand to answer questions. Once outside, take a few minutes to stroll a self-guided path through the nature garden next to the building. Common plants are identified, including bur sage, desert willow, and creosote bush. In spring the latter sprouts puffy white buds reminiscent of pussy willows before blooming in yellow flowers.

The well-marked auto route through the park offers plenty of pullouts for photographing the beautiful rock formations, whose colors range from egg white to deep red to indigo black. A popular hike is the half-mile self-guided nature trail through a narrow painted canyon to Mouses Tank, named for a natural cistern used by a legendary Paiute fleeing a posse in the 1890s. Suspected of committing a variety of crimes from petty theft to murder, he was eventually hunted down and shot to death.

The trail to his cistern winds through a canyon marked with petroglyphic symbols of animals and other designs, the legacy of earlier Native Americans who occupied these parts thousands of years ago. Prehistoric residents of the valley include the Basket Maker people and later the Anasazi Pueblo farmers from the nearby fertile Moapa valley. Keep an eye out for wildlife. The curious S-shaped markings on the sandy trail are probably left by sidewinder snakes. Greater

---

Right: *The light of late evening—when the deep earth tones take on the intensity of the last rays of the sun—casts dark shadows into the jumbled tumble of ancient golden rocks at Valley of Fire State Park.*

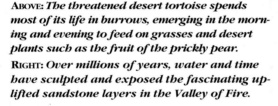

ABOVE: *The threatened desert tortoise spends most of its life in burrows, emerging in the morning and evening to feed on grasses and desert plants such as the fruit of the prickly pear.*
RIGHT: *Over millions of years, water and time have sculpted and exposed the fascinating uplifted sandstone layers in the Valley of Fire.*

roadrunners also use the trail while ravens, house finches, sage sparrows, and many migrant birds flit along the canyon rim and bushes. Chuckwallas, vegetarian lizards, perch on ledges and boulders; at the first sign of predators, they crawl into the nearest crack and puff up so they can't be dislodged.

Just past the trail to Mouses Tank lies Rainbow Vista, a favorite photographic point because it provides panoramic view of multicolored sandstone. From here an easy three-mile round-trip walk leads to an excellent vantage point for viewing the deep red sandstone of Fire Canyon and the unique geologic features of Silica Dome. A longer hike (seven miles round-trip) goes to White Domes.

Head west through the park to examine the many Indian petroglyphs at Atlatl Rock, named for the rock-art depiction of a notched stick used to throw spears. Nearby is a short interpretative trail leading to a collection of petrified logs that washed into the area from ancient

forests 225 million years ago—a telling reminder of the great changes that have occurred in this unusual corner of the globe.

Continue west on Route 169, turn west on Interstate 15, and then quickly turn onto Route 168 north and west, taking the Warm Springs Road cutoff to **Moapa Valley National Wildlife Refuge❖.** This postage-stamp–size preserve provides 31 acres of protected habitat for the endangered Moapa dace, a small fish once commonly found throughout thermal springs forming the headwaters of the Muddy River. The fish is now threatened due to habitat destruction and competition from introduced (exotic) species. Other federal candidates for threatened or endangered status include the Moapa White River springfish, the Moapa roundtail chub, and the Moapa speckled dace.

Although established in 1979, the refuge is still in the developmental stages as habitat restoration efforts continue. The site is notable for its large stand of fan palms and date palms along the river. Thousands of

The Pahranagat National Wildlife Refuge provides vital wetland habitat for migrating waterfowl such as the northern pintail duck (bottom right). Coveys of Gambel's quail (top right) roam the desert thickets, and shorebirds such as the American avocet (above) are occasional visitors.

years ago a branch of the Anasazi civilization blossomed here. Later European settlers diverted the water for agricultural use, creating problems for resident wildlife. Other sensitive species include ringtail cats, Moapa pebblesnails, White River snails, and an endemic riffle beetle.

To reach the larger and more established **Pahranagat National Wildlife Refuge❖,** follow Route 168 to Route 93 and turn north. Flanking the highway, this narrow valley contains two large lakes that provide a sanctuary for some 193 species of birds. The refuge's 5,380 acres of marshes, open water, cottonwood-lined shore, and native grass meadows are truly an oasis. (The name Pahranagat comes from the Paiute word meaning "place of many waters.") Shorebirds such as egrets, great blue herons, black-necked stilts, greater yellowlegs, long-billed curlews, and four kinds of sandpiper congregate along the edges of both lakes. In fall the waters attract migrating waterfowl, including tundra swans, Canada geese, mallard, northern pintail, and ruddy ducks.

Rafts of pied-billed grebes, migrating American white pelicans, and ring-billed gulls ply the open water. Keep binoculars handy for viewing the upland areas, where numerous species of flycatcher, swallow, wren, and sparrow feed. The songs of 14 different kinds of warblers fill the air, offering a marked contrast to the usually quiet desert. The abundant birds attract plenty of raptors, including northern harriers,

210

ABOVE RIGHT: *The western meadowlark's melodious song fills the air at the Pahranagat refuge year-round.*

sharp-shinned hawks, ferruginous hawks, golden and bald eagles, and endangered peregrine falcons. The birdlife is so rich that the Audubon Society sponsors field trips here at least twice a year.

Another 76 miles north on Route 93 near the town of Panaca is **Cathedral Gorge State Park❖.** The 1,600-acre park occupies a narrow valley lined with heavily eroded cliffs of bentonite clay that look like flying buttresses on a Gothic cathedral and range from white to mocha. A million years ago this area was covered by a freshwater lake. As in modern-day lakes, sediments and gravel piled on the lake floor. When the climate changed and the water drained, erosion shaped the sediments, carving rivulets in the siltstone and clay shale formations.

The sightly spires, gullies, fans, and gorges have been attracting visitors for generations, and during the 1920s they were used as backdrops for open-air vaudevilles. The area was named a state park in 1935. Along several short self-guided nature trails are signs offering detailed descriptions of the biological processes working here and fine opportunities for wildlife viewing. An excellent overview can be found at Miller Point, two miles farther north on Route 93, where dune primroses and Indian ricegrass grow on small sand dunes along the edges of the eroded escarpment while narrowleaf yucca, juniper tree, barberry, greasewood, and four-wing saltbush sprout in the middle of the valley.

211

Although deer browse here during the late fall and winter, most of the mammals are small, such as black-tailed jackrabbits, coyotes, skunks, kit foxes, and kangaroo rats. Resident birds include ravens, kestrels, black-throated sparrows, and rock wrens. Migrant tanagers, bluebirds, warblers, and hummingbirds add even more hues to the colorful gorge.

GREAT BASIN NATIONAL PARK

Nevada is home to one of America's newer national parks. To reach **Great Basin National Park❖,** continue about 160 miles north on Route 93 through a long basin, Lake Valley, which is bordered on both sides by mountain ranges, the North Pahrock and Egan ranges on the west and the Wilson Creek and Fortification on the east. The drive reveals Nevada's famous basin and range topography, the washboardlike pattern of mountain and valley, mountain and valley that covers the entire state. Lake Valley is a patchwork quilt of sagebrush and cultivated grass where a close look at the cows often reveals pronghorn grazing right alongside them. At the north end of the valley more mountains hove into view, the Schell Creek Range to the west and the Snake Range to the east. Of the 13 peaks rising above 11,000 feet in the Snake, the two highest are 13,063-foot **Wheeler Peak** and 12,050-foot **Mount Moriah.** Follow Route 50 east between this cloud-scraping pair and over 7,154-foot Sacramento Pass to reach the park entrance near the town of Baker via Routes 487 and 488.

Great Basin National Park, Nevada's only one, was established in 1986, but its national protection status dates back to 1922, when a portion of the area was set aside as Lehman Caves National Monument. The story of **Lehman Caves** began more than 500 million years ago, when the land was covered by a shallow sea. Over time the shells and bones of creatures living in the warm, shallow waters landed on the seafloor, where they piled up in a layer of calcium carbonate, or limestone, thousands of feet thick. Twenty million years ago, long after the sea had disappeared, the collision between the earth's plates caused the continent to break into blocks along fault lines running north and south. Some blocks sank while

---

RIGHT: *Bentonite clay cliffs are the centerpiece of the aptly named Cathedral Gorge State Park, where flying buttresses and gothic spires are testaments to the power of eons of rain and water runoff.*

others rose. The Snake Range is one that tilted upward. Sometime either before or after the mountains rose (geologists aren't certain when), a mass of molten rock pushed through cracks in the rock layers beneath Wheeler Peak, changing some of the limestone into marble. Next, runoff from rain and snow removed thousands of feet of sediment and widened the cracks even more, forming caverns.

In 1869 a down-on-his-luck gold prospector named Absalom Lehman established a ranch near the base of Wheeler Peak. In 1885, while poking around the mountain two miles above his house, he discovered the opening to a wondrous cavern. News of the discovery spread fast, and before long Lehman was charging visitors a dollar for a candle and permission to enter the cavern. (The fare included his promise to come looking for them if they hadn't returned by an agreed-upon hour!) After several changes in proprietorship, the National Park Service gained control of the cave in 1922.

Inside the mountain is a huge quarter-mile-long cavern richly deco-

ABOVE: *The black-tailed jackrabbit, with its giant ears, lives in open brushy areas where it covers the ground in impressive ten-foot hops.*
LEFT: *In the 1920s open-air vaudeville performances were staged in the rock-strewn natural amphitheaters of Cathedral Gorge.*

rated with speleotherms—better known as stalactites, stalagmites, columns, draperies, and flowstone. Lehman Caves is famous for its delicate and interesting rarities, including shields—mysterious structures that consist of two roughly circular halves and look like flattened clamshells. Other eye-catching features are helectites, which resemble chow mein noodles; cave popcorn, which looks like its namesake; and clusters of snow-white needles called aragonite.

At the entrance to Lehman Caves, the Park Service operates a visitor center that provides an introduction to the natural history of the 77,100-acre park. Don't miss the wonderful slide show, which includes breathtaking images of the national park in all its seasonal colors.

From the visitor center, head up **Wheeler Peak Scenic Drive,** a 12-

OVERLEAF: *Flanked by mounds of yellow rabbitbrush, a cattle guard in Great Basin National Park prevents livestock that graze in surrounding rangelands from gaining access to the areas reserved for wildlife.*

ABOVE: *The plant community along Baker Creek in Great Basin National Park includes sagebrush, rabbitbrush, pinyon pine, juniper, willow, and cottonwood, which support a diverse wildlife population.*

mile auto tour that gains 3,400 feet in elevation and passes through a staircase of habitats along the way. The road rises quickly, traversing the first life zone of pinyon-juniper woodland, which features a most attractive shrub, the cliff rose. Its creamy yellow flowers resemble small wild roses but smell more like orange blossoms. The Native Americans who inhabited the region made clothing from the plant's bark (archaeological evidence shows that human habitation here goes back thousands of years), and deer depend on it for winter browse.

As the road climbs, the pinyons and junipers give way to the aspens lining Lehman Creek; their leaves are especially colorful during the spring and fall. In spring the glacier-fed freshet swells with runoff, becoming a boisterous ribbon of white water as it tumbles down its rocky bed. After passing through thickets of shrubby mountain mahogany and manzanita dotted with pink- and yellow-flowered prickly-pear cactus, the road penetrates a deep forest of Engelmann spruce and Douglas fir. It winds up at Wheeler Peak Campground in a subalpine forest of limber pine and spruce, an ear-popping 9,950 feet above sea level.

Leave the car behind and follow the trails to view **Wheeler Peak** and the year-round sheet of ice draped around it like an ermine cloak. This remnant glacier—the only one of its kind in the Great Basin—is a

ABOVE: *The 13,000-foot summit of Wheeler Peak dominates a snowy land-scape in Great Basin National Park. A grove of slender aspens seems to huddle behind a stand of darker pines to ward off winter's cold.*

legacy of the Ice Age. Other reminders of the alpine glaciers that once capped all the peaks above 9,000 feet can be found in the piles of boulders, sand, and gravel called glacial till that were pushed up to form ridges and mounds and in the sparkling lakes that fill the many cirques gouged out by ice.

Near the parking lot is a grove of ancient bristlecone pines, gnarled Methuselahs that are the stuff of legends. Most of the trees growing here are 2,000 to 3,000 years old. One is even older: The Prometheus tree was dated at 4,950 years old—1,200 years older than the Egyptian pyramids! Bristlecones grow slowly, and needles can live 40 years. The taller they are, the older they're apt to be. As Ronald Lanner writes in his poetic tome *Trees of the Great Basin,* when it comes to bristlecones, "Adversity breeds longevity."

Flower-spangled meadows carpet the mountain at the tree line. Among the more showy species are buttercups, Fremont geraniums, violets, blazing stars, shooting stars, bluebells, Indian paintbrush, monkeyflowers, pussytoes, asters, and tansy mustard. The park is also rich in animal life. In the air turkey vultures, red-tailed hawks, golden eagles, and rough-legged hawks search for prey, and blue and sage grouse, California quail, and chukars scurry at ground level. Northern flickers,

yellow-bellied sapsuckers, and hairy woodpeckers tap the bark on trees while brown creepers and Clark's nut-crackers search their trunks and limbs. Olive-sided flycatchers, Say's phoebes, and violet-green swallows dart after fly-ing insects, and northern orioles, evening grosbeaks, lazuli buntings, pine siskins, and yellow-breasted chats light up the sky with a rainbow of feathered radiance. Mammalian species are also well represented within the park: Coyotes, short-tail weasels, and bobcats prowl for a variety of prey ranging from black-tailed jackrabbits to pocket mice, from ground squirrels to northern pocket gophers.

ABOVE: *Named for a nineteenth century botanist, the pretty but rank-smelling Parry's prim-rose grows in high country at the edge of streams or snow-fields and blooms in July.*

LEFT: *In the southern reaches of Great Basin National Park stands mysterious Lexington Arch. When the wind whistles through, the arch sounds like an instrument played by gods.*

Wheeler Peak offers many high-al-titude climbs and hiking trails. Al-though the area right around the peak is the most visited, don't miss the ex-treme southern part of the park. Just below the visitor center, head south on Baker Road, then west up to 7,500 feet through pinyons and aspens to Baker Creek Campground. A six-mile hike on the Baker Lake and Johnson Lake Loop trails leads to a pair of scenic alpine lakes.

Rising above the floor of Lexington Canyon at the southern tip of the park is imposing **Lexington Arch,** a six-story bridgelike span different from other arches in the Southwest because it is made of limestone rather than the more easily sculpted sandstone. Geologists speculate that it was once a passage in a cave system like the ones beneath Wheeler Peak. The presence of flowstone, a smooth, glossy deposit that forms in caves, at the base of the opening supports their theory. Whatever its origin, Lexington Arch is a natural spectacle guaranteed to awe and inspire.

From Great Basin, take Route 50 west toward the town of Ely. While

ABOVE: *The bristlecone pines atop Wheeler Peak are amazing relics of the past: one tree, said to be the world's oldest living thing, is nearly*

crossing the Schell Creek Range, turn north on the road signed to **Cave Lake State Park❖,** a dam-created 32-acre lake at 7,300 feet. With picnicking and camping, the park is a convenient base for summer hikes and winter cross-country ski trips into the surrounding Humboldt National Forest.

From the park, the road north turns to dirt and winds its way through the heart of the 53-mile-long **Schell Creek Range,** which lies within the **Humboldt National Forest.** Presiding over the range are 11,890-foot-high North Schell and 11,765-foot-high South Schell peaks,

5,000 years old. The hardy, stiff-needled conifers grow only above 7,000 feet, exposed to wind, sun, and extreme cold.

a towering pair making the range the fourth-highest in the state. More than a dozen streams cascade down through forests of Douglas fir, Engelmann spruce, aspen, and cottonwood. Bristlecone pines grow near the tree line; above that, alpine tundra and then bare rock take over. Atop the peaks the weather is cool even in summer, and in winter the way is blocked by snow. Whatever the season, one thing is certain: Any visit to the Schell Creek Range is apt to be uncrowded. Few people come here to explore and enjoy the sweeping vistas of Nevada's basin and range that the peaks provide.

223

NORTHERN NEVADA

N orthern Nevada is a land of sharp contrasts that can't seem to decide whether it's a mountain state or a desert one. A 150-mile line from Lake Tahoe on the California border northeast to the Black Rock Desert captures this quest for identity: It connects the largest alpine lake on the continent with one of the flattest, driest, most lunarlike surfaces on earth. In between are lush pine forests, snowcapped peaks more than 10,000 feet high, a booming city full of jangling neon-lit casinos, sagebrush-covered scrublands, and the last vestige of a prehistoric inland sea bigger than Lake Ontario.

From Mount Rose near the California line, the view east is a series of north-south mountain ranges alternating with north-south basins all the way across the state to Utah. This pattern of peak and valley, peak and valley has a cadence all its own, as captured by the writer John McPhee in his poetic homage to Nevada's geology, *Basin and Range*:

> Basin. Fault. Range. Basin. Fault. Range. A mile of relief between basin and range. Stillwater Range. Pleasant Valley. Tobin Range. Jersey Valley. Sonoma Range. Pumpernickel Valley. Shoshone Range. Reese River Valley. Pequop Mountains. Steptoe Valley. Ondographic rhythms of Basin and Range.

LEFT: *In the mountains of northeastern Nevada, purple-flowered penstemon lends a regal air to a lush aspen-lined meadow that skirts the volcanic cliffs of Marys River Basin in the Jarbidge Wilderness.*

Reno is surrounded by a Whitman's Sampler of geography, geology, and biological genealogy. Huge Lahontan cutthroat trout whose ancestors date back to Pleistocene times ply the waters of Pyramid Lake. Stillwater Marsh provides refuge for thousands of migratory waterfowl and songbirds. Black bears, mountain lions, and elusive Sierra Nevada red foxes prowl the forests above Lake Tahoe–Nevada State Park.

Head east from Reno on Route 50, dubbed the "loneliest highway in the world," and watch the secrets of the basin and range reveal themselves in a long, slow reverie. Drive across a sea of sagebrush where movement can be sensed only by the passing of shadows created by drifting clouds. Visit a real-life Triassic Park, the Berlin-Ichthyosaur fossil beds, which contain the remains of a fierce marine dinosaur. Hike into the Table Mountain Wilderness in the Monitor Range to see where Rocky Mountain elk once again migrate. Climb Ruby Dome in the Ruby Mountains. Like rungs of some biological ladder, each step of the way brings a whole new assemblage of fauna. Pinyon-juniper gives way to aspen to Jeffrey pine to limber pine to alpine tundra.

Northern Nevada contains some of the remotest countryside anywhere. The Jarbidge Wilderness in the northeastern corner can be reached only by driving mile after mile on a spine-jarring, white-knuckle dirt road—but the reward is worth it. Crystal springs bubble out of a mountain range capped by snow, dotted with alpine lakes and wildflower-strewn meadows, and draped by subalpine fir and aspen trees. All the way across the state in the northwestern corner lies an even more isolated landscape, where the bleak flattop tablelands of the Sheldon National Wildlife Refuge adjoin the barren silt playa of the Black Rock Desert. Though often overlooked and seldom visited, each has an incredible story to tell.

The itinerary through northern Nevada begins by circling Reno to visit the state's remnant ancient lakes—Pyramid Lake, Stillwater Marsh, and Walker Lake. Next it follows Route 50 east for a glimpse of the basins and ranges that line the breadth of the state like ribs, stopping at a fossil bed where seagoing dinosaurs rest their bones. Turning north,

---

Overleaf: *This distinctively shaped formation was an island floating in an emerald sea when explorer John C. Frémont named Pyramid Lake in 1844. Today water levels are lower and landforms have changed.*

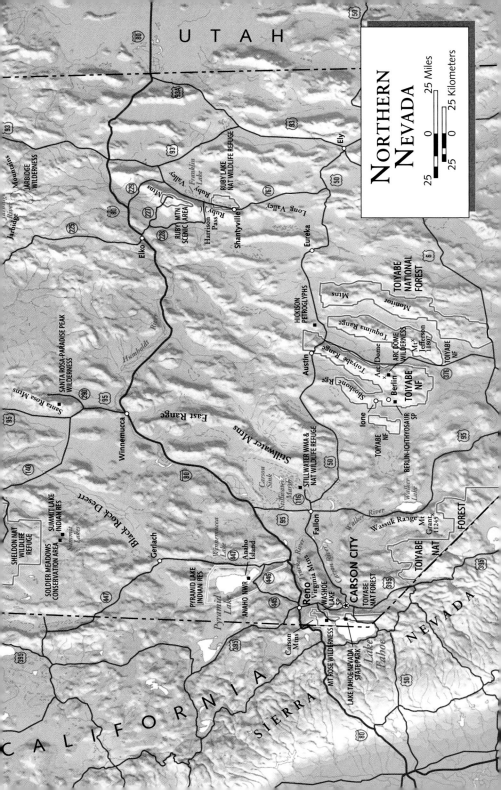

Jarbidge River Mtns
Jarbidge
ARBIDGE
WILDERNESS

RUBY LAKE
NAT WILDLIFE REFUGE

Ruby Valley
Franklin Lake
Ruby Mtns
RUBY MTN
SCENIC
AREA
Harrison
Pass
Shantyville

Long Valley

Ely

Eureka

Elko

Santa Rosa Mtns
SANTA ROSA-PARADISE PEAK
WILDERNESS

TOIYABE
NATIONAL
FOREST

HICKISON
PETROGLYPHS

Monitor Mtns

Toquima Range

Arc Dome
ARC DOME
WILDERNESS
Mt
Jefferson
11807

TOIYABE
NF

Humboldt River

East Range

Winnemucca

Austin

Toiyabe Range

Shoshone Range

Berlin
TOIYABE
NF

Ione

TOIYABE
NF

BERLIN-ICHTHYOSAUR
SP

Stillwater Mtns

Carson
Sink

STILLWATER WMA &
NAT WILDLIFE REFUGE

Walker Lake

SHELDON NAT
WILDLIFE
REFUGE

SUMMIT
LAKE
INDIAN RES

SOLDIER MEADOWS
CONSERVATION AREA

Summit
Lakes

Black Rock Desert

Gerlach

Stillwater
Marsh

Fallon

Walker River

Wassuk Range

Mt
Grant
11245

TOIYABE
NAT
FOREST

PYRAMID LAKE
INDIAN RES

Winnemucca
Lake

Anaho
Island

ANAHO NWR

Pyramid
Lake

Truckee River

Reno
Virginia Mtns
WASHOE
LAKE
SP

CARSON CITY

Carson River

TOIYABE
NAT FOREST

CALIFORNIA

Carson
Mtns

MT ROSE WILDERNESS

LAKE TAHOE-NEVADA
STATE PARK

Lake
Tahoe

NEVADA

SIERRA

the route passes the Ruby Mountains and the vast Jarbidge Wilderness, then travels west to the Santa Rosa Mountains, the sprawling Sheldon National Wildlife Refuge, and the eerie emptiness of the Black Rock Desert in the northwestern corner of the state.

RENO AND ENVIRONS

Reno calls itself the "biggest little city in the world," and indeed some of the state's biggest natural attractions are within an hour's drive of downtown. Thirty-five miles north on Route 445 is the "littlest-known big lake" in the western United States. **Pyramid Lake❖** is 28 miles long, 11 miles wide, and 370 feet at its deepest. It was nearly 75 times bigger and 10 times deeper 50,000 years ago, when it was part of the enormous Lake Lahontan, a prehistoric freshwater inland great lake that spread across the entire northwestern third of the state. With the retreat of the last Ice Age, Lake Lahontan began to disappear, evaporating in the warmer, drier climate like a backyard puddle in July.

The lake was named by explorer John C. Frémont, who passed by in 1844. After trekking through the desert on his way back from Oregon, the intrepid Frémont climbed a rocky promontory and saw a sheet of green water surrounded by nearly barren gray and pink hills that "broke upon our eyes like the ocean." Near the shoreline was an island with a profile like that of the great Pyramid of Cheops.

Frémont was not the first human to set eyes on the lake. Eleven thousand years ago prehistoric people lived in caves in the tufa formations overlooking the lake, weaving baskets of tule and spearing fish along its shallow shores. Later, the Northern Paiute people moved into the area, attracted by the lake's two endemic fish species, the cui-ui—a prehistoric sucker that dates back tens of thousands of years—and the gigantic Lahontan cutthroat trout—a landlocked king salmon that averages 30 to 35 pounds.

The Northern Paiute still live at Pyramid Lake. Along with the surrounding desert lands, it was designated the 400,000-acre Pyramid Lake Indian Reservation by President Ulysses S. Grant in 1874 after nonnative settlers triggered a brief war by kidnapping several local Native American women.

Other skirmishes—over control of water—have plagued the desert lake ever since. Pyramid Lake is fed by the Truckee River, which

ABOVE: *As silent and mysterious as the sphinx, the Stone Mother forma-tion on the shores of Pyramid Lake—now home to shorebirds and waterfowl—is mute testimony to the region's violent geologic past.*

rises at populated Lake Tahoe and passes through Reno. Reclamation projects and upstream development have diverted more than half the water flowing into the emerald green lake, and as a result its surface has dropped almost a hundred feet in the past century. Lower lake levels and the construction of a dam on the Truckee River near the town of Nixon have helped push the native cui-ui and Lahontan cutthroat to the brink of extinction. The sucker is classified as endangered and the trout as threatened.

The loss of water has affected other wildlife as well. Anaho Island in Pyramid Lake attracts many species of waterfowl and shorebirds, including Canada geese, California gulls, Caspian terns, double-crested cormorants, and eared and western grebes. President Woodrow Wilson named it a bird sanctuary in 1913. Now known as the 750-acre **Anaho National Wildlife Refuge❖,** the island was historically a breeding ground for the country's largest colony of American white pelicans.

231

ABOVE: *At Pyramid Lake, white pelicans disappeared as the habitat changed; experts hope to induce the birds to return to their longtime rookery.*
RIGHT: *Yellow bee plant, a desert wildflower with petals the color of the sun, sways in a stiff breeze on the sage-covered basins north of Nixon.*

Each spring for centuries 10,000 pairs of these magnificent white birds with black-tipped wings spanning 10 feet migrated to the desert island from their winter homes in southern California and Mexico. Females gave birth to their young while males flew to nearby Winnemucca Lake to fish for tui chub and carp. In 1940 Winnemucca Lake dried up, and the fish in Stillwater Marsh, 60 miles to the east, nearly disappeared as well. Diminishing food supplies caused a dramatic decline in the number of nesting pairs of pelicans, which dropped to an all-time low of nine in 1991. Efforts are now under way

to bring back not only the pelicans, but the cui-ui and Lahontan cut-throat as well. A fish hatchery at Pyramid Lake raises 500,000 trout for release each year. In addition, water users are trying to devise a more equitable arrangement for managing Pyramid Lake's water supply.

In the meantime, visitors can still find plenty to see and do here. Fishing for cutthroat is a popular pastime, as is scanning the cotton-woods and willows that line the mouth of the Truckee River. Golden eagles are common all year, and in spring, birds by the thousands con-gregate here. Raptors take to the air in search of prey while songbirds

Above: *Photographer Timothy O'Sullivan converted a Civil War army ambulance into a mule-drawn darkroom for the 1868 King Survey of the 40th parallel; here he documented his equipment near Carson Sink.*

perch on the branches calling to one another. And the surface of the lake at the mouth of the river looks like fallen snow when pelicans, gulls, and other waterfowl form huge rafts as they wait for fish to enter.

Included in the water negotiations for Pyramid Lake is the well-being of the marshes at **Stillwater National Wildlife Refuge❖** and **Stillwater Wildlife Management Area** near Fallon. This 162,000-acre area east of Reno via Routes 50 and 116 was also covered by Lake Lahontan thousands of years ago. Today it is part of the Carson Sink, a shallow depression in the sage- and alkali-covered scrub where the Carson River trickles to its end.

The Stillwater Wildlife Management Area encompasses the largest marsh in Nevada, a principal stopover on the vital Pacific Flyway migratory route. Prior to this century the marshes here were lush and robust, attracting ducks, geese, and swans by the hundreds of thousands. For centuries Native Americans relied on the desert wetlands, living off the ample wildlife and making food, clothes, and shelter from the aquatic plants. In one of the more interesting uses of native plants, they shaped tule and cattails into unique floats, which they "rode" into open water and used as blinds for fishing and hunting.

After water was diverted for agricultural use in the early 1900s, the sloughs and marshes nearly disappeared. Alarmed, state and federal agencies joined forces in the 1940s to restore some of the original habitat. The acreage restored fluctuates from year to year. From 1950 to 1970 approximately 34,000 acres have been revived. More restoration is under way, including an ambitious project by the Nature Conservancy and federal agencies to supplement Stillwater Marsh with water from the Carson and Truckee rivers.

When water is available—historically in spring but in recent years in fall—ten large impoundments are filled, attracting flocks of migratory waterfowl. During peak times as many as 250,000 mallard, gadwall, pintail, green-winged teal, redhead, and canvasback ducks; 6,000 Canada and snow geese; and 12,000 tundra swans have been counted here. Shorebirds include snowy egrets, white-faced ibis, great blue and black-crowned night herons, American avocets, black-necked stilts, Wilson's phalaropes, and long-billed dowitchers. Virginia rails, killdeers, and soras prod for food along the muddy shores while marsh wrens, yellow-headed blackbirds, yellow warblers, and cliff swallows flit over the tule and saltbush.

A 26-mile auto tour winds its way around the impoundments and over dike roads along sloughs and canals in a landscape of sand dunes, the sprawling Carson Sink, and the volcanic Stillwater Mountains. Although most of the region is covered by greasewood and saltbush, spring rains sprout primroses and sand verbena. Horned toads and other lizards abound while coyotes prowl for black-tailed jackrabbits and Great Basin kangaroo rats. Northern harriers, kestrels, and barn and short-eared owls can be spotted hovering overhead. In dry times (most of the year), the sunbaked, alkali-kissed refuge is silent and seemingly devoid of life.

Another vestige of Lake Lahontan can be found about 60 miles south (return to Route 50 and take Route 95 south at the town of

Fallon). Deep blue 38,500-acre **Walker Lake❖** provides a welcome visual relief in the otherwise monochromatic desert landscape. Its waters have been beckoning visitors for centuries. In the 1820s frontier explorers Jedediah Smith and Peter Skene Ogden drank their fill, and a decade later the water saved the life of a fellow trailblazer dying of thirst, "Walkin'" Joe Walker, the fur trapper and mapping expedition leader made famous by New York columnist Washington Irving.

Walker's namesake lake shares Pyramid Lake's ancestral waters, as well as its diminishing numbers of Lahontan cutthroat trout and declining water level. In less than a century, water diversion for agriculture and development has lowered the lake's surface by more than 85 feet, and a dam and reservoir built on the Walker River in the 1930s stopped the annual spawning runs of native trout. Nowadays the Nevada Division of Wildlife must stock the lake with fingerlings raised at the Pyramid Lake hatchery.

Still, Walker Lake is a natural wonderland. It boasts a beautiful high-desert setting whose sandy beaches and shallow waters along the shore attract snowy plover, American avocets, and black-necked stilts. Harlequin ducks, brant, American white pelicans, snow geese, and old-squaws come by the hundreds. Providing a rugged mountain backdrop to the west is the Wassuk Range, a stretch of mountains etched with wooded canyons. Sentinel over the desert lake is 11,239-foot-high **Mount Grant,** a bead in the sights for viewing the granite escarpment of the Sierra Nevada 50 miles farther west.

LAKE TAHOE

In these parts the Sierra Nevada is the boundary between California and Nevada, and although California claims much of the range's land mass, a portion spills into the Silver State at Lake Tahoe. The lake, in fact, is split between the states, although Nevada claims only 29 miles of its 72-mile shoreline. The water in Lake Tahoe, the largest alpine lake on the continent, is so translucent that objects down 150 feet or more on the bottom can be clearly seen.

Tahoe's beauty has not gone unnoticed. Eight hundred years ago

RIGHT: *The rugged crest of the Wassuk Range to the west and the billowy clouds overhead are painted by the setting sun, as the still, shallow waters of Walker Lake sink into the darkness of night.*

Nevada's state bird, the mountain bluebird (above left), inhabits both timberline meadows and sagebrush plains. Emerald Bay State Park (above right) occupies one of the most scenic sections of Lake Tahoe.

Washoe Indians gathered on its shores to catch trout and enjoy its splendors, and today it attracts visitors by the million. Although there has been a great deal of building to accommodate them all, primarily at the southern and northern tips and along the California side, much of Nevada's shoreline remains undeveloped, including three miles protected as **Lake Tahoe–Nevada State Park❖.**

The park encompasses 13,468 acres of lakeshore and forested mountains. The lake side of the park—Sand Harbor—gets ample use in summers, and the mountain side offers wilderness settings. Trails lead to four more bodies of water found within the park's borders: 380-acre Marlette Lake, 90-acre Spooner Lake, and the smaller Twin Lakes and Hobart Creek Reservoir. Along the way, hikers pass through forests of ponderosa, Jeffrey, and limber pines. Other trees growing from 6,200 to 8,850 feet include white fir, incense cedar, aspen, and red fir. In spring and summer the meadows are spangled with colorful wildflowers as

238

RIGHT: *These pink wildflowers are called elephant heads because each flower forms a perfect pachyderm head—ears, trunk, and all.*

baby blue-eyes, peonies, snow plant, blue flax, lupines, columbine, shooting stars, and Indian paintbrush add to nature's palette.

Many visitors come to enjoy the wildlife. Birders can spot numerous species, including mallard, mergansers, spotted sandpipers, soras, and ospreys at water's edge and Steller's jays, Clark's nutcrackers, and mountain chickadees in the woods. Producing the tap-tap-tap on trees are a variety of cavity dwellers, including northern flickers, Williamson's sapsuckers, and Lewis's, downy, white-headed, and hairy woodpeckers. Mountain bluebirds, western tanagers, yellow-rumped warblers, lazuli buntings, and ruby-crowned kinglets

240

paint the forest sky. Although golden-mantled ground squirrels, mule deer, and marmots are easy to find, harder to glimpse are bobcats, mountain lions, and black bears. Even more elusive is the endemic Sierra Nevada red fox.

The park enjoys plenty of wildlife because it adjoins the far-flung **Toiyabe National Forest✧,** the largest one in the contiguous United States. The Toiyabe's Carson Ranger District manages nearly 72,000 acres on the Nevada side of Lake Tahoe. Just northeast of the lake via Route 431 rises a 10,778-foot peak that is the centerpiece of the officially designated **Mount Rose Wilderness✧.** Trails to the summit offer stunning views of Lake Tahoe and the steep mountains to the west and of Reno and the Great Basin to the east.

Galena Creek roars down the heavily forested mountain, lending its name to 400-acre **Galena Creek Park✧.** Here the creek is lined with manzanita, cottonwood, willow, alder, and dogwood, and away from the river grows ponderosa pine. The sweet smell of vanilla wafting through the forest on warm summer days comes from Jeffrey pine. Foraging for food in the understory are rufous-sided towhees, golden-mantled ground squirrels, and raccoon. In the summer, when the bitter cherry is in fruit, keep a lookout for black bears—they love the stuff.

In the Washoe Valley off Route 395 between Carson City and Reno lies **Washoe Lake State Park✧,** bordered by the Carson and Virginia ranges on the west and east, respectively. Although snowmelt in the

ABOVE: *Tawny bobcats turn gray in winter without losing their distinctive black spots. North America's most common wildcat was named for its stubby, or "bobbed," tail.*

LEFT: *Seen from Toiyabe National Forest, Nevada's tallest mountain, Boundary Peak, shimmers in the distance, still lightly dusted with winter snow.*

OVERLEAF: *Clumps of silvery sage and feathery golden desert grasses intermingle with lichen-festooned volcanic boulders at the Grimes Point Archaeological Area near Fallon.*

Top Left: *Cinnamon teal spice up wetlands throughout Nevada; males turn nearly red while in breeding plumage.*

Bottom Left: *Marked by its striking red eyes and golden ear tufts, the gregarious eared grebe uses a floating nest.*

Right: *When courting, male sandhill cranes perform eye-catching aerial jumps in an effort to woo mates. Their long, rolling calls can carry more than a mile.*

Carson Mountains provides much of its water, the 5,700-acre lake has high alkalinity, which doesn't seem to bother the resident wildlife. White bass, catfish, carp, and perch swim in its waters, and a variety of waterfowl and shorebirds flock here during migration. A few small islands in the lake provide safe refuge for nesting species such as sandhill cranes, great blue herons, white-faced ibis, American white pelicans, American coots, and various types of ducks. Muskrats and beavers make their home in the lake while mule deer graze onshore. Because the park is a popular outing for nearby residents, summer weekends are apt to be crowded.

CENTRAL MOUNTAINS AND VALLEYS

Signs, locals, and even chambers of commerce freely admit that Route 50, which stretches clear across Nevada from Stateline on the California border at Lake Tahoe to the Utah line, is the "loneliest highway in the world." Most out-of-state visitors who drive it will agree. The biggest town between Fallon and Ely—a distance of 257 miles—is Eureka, population 500. The highway mimics the terrain: hills and downgrades broken by long, flat straightaways. This part of Nevada is the quintessence of basin and range topography—a landscape shaped to resemble ripples on a pond by the clash of continental plates 400 miles to the west.

One hundred ten miles east of Fallon Route 50 cuts across the tops of four parallel sections of the **Toiyabe National Forest❖.** On a

road map this foursome, running north to south, looks like green claw marks scratched in the middle of the state. The marks represent the contours of four parallel mountain ranges—the Shoshone, Toiyabe, Toquima, and Monitor—separating long valleys, or basins. Each range is worth a visit.

Traveling from west to east, the first stop is the **Shoshone Mountains,** reached by a gravel road running south from Austin and signed "Ione, 43 miles." Between 1881 and 1886 stagecoaches traveled this road—then known as the Austin to Grantsville stage route. Just beyond Ione is **Berlin-Ichthyosaur State Park**❖. Berlin, one of the best-preserved ghost towns in Nevada, was a booming gold- and silver-mining town with a population of 200 to 250 during its heyday at the turn of the century. About 225 million years earlier it was the shore of a vast inland sea inhabited by ichthyosaurs, mighty 60-foot-long marine predators weighing 35 tons. Scores of them were

trapped along the shores of the sea as it began to shrink. Although they could breathe out of water—they had lungs like whales—they were doomed when the water disappeared because they suffocated under their own weight.

A Stanford University geologist uncovered the fossilized remains of these giant beasts in 1928 while looking for fossils of ammonites, extinct cephalopods abundant in the Mesozoic era. Excavation that continued on and off for the next 30 years eventually unearthed 40 ichthyosaurs, 3 of which are on display. (The visitor center provides more information.) A three-mile interpretative trail leads through handsome country peppered with pinyon-juniper and rabbitbrush and in spring, numerous wildflower species. Keep an eye out for reptiles of another sort, namely western rattlesnakes.

ABOVE: *A good swimmer, agile jumper, and superb rock climber, the Rocky Mountain bighorn sheep frequents alpine meadows in high, undisturbed areas, such as Nevada's Ruby Mountains.*

LEFT: *Each autumn large stands of golden-leaved aspens (each growing from a single root system) light up the walls of Lamoille Canyon in the Ruby Mountains, making this area a favorite among hikers.*

From the same gravel road between Austin and Ione, turn east into the **Toiyabe Range,** where 50 miles of the sharp 125-mile spine-like range are above the 10,000-foot marker. On the east side it is dissected by numerous rocky canyons. The **Arc Dome Wilderness❖,** Nevada's largest, occupies 115,000 acres here. In spring 40 different species of nesting birds, including red-naped sapsuckers and northern flickers, can be seen from Camp Columbine, a U.S. Forest Service campground. A colony of Belding's ground squirrels inhabit a labyrinthine system of burrows nearby, attracting such predators as prairie falcons, northern goshawks, and coyotes. Trails from the camp to the top of 11,775-foot Arc Dome lead through the state's largest stand of limber pine, where blue grouse forage. The rockier, higher elevation is home to desert bighorn sheep, mountain lions, and bobcats, and occasionally, migrating Rocky Mountain elk pass through.

To proceed to the **Toquima Range,** return to Route 50 and turn south on Route 376 12 miles past Austin. This range is capped by 11,949-foot **Mount Jefferson,** actually a collection of three summits spread across an 8-mile-long ridge about 11,000 feet above sea level. On a clear day hikers can see Mount Rose above Reno, the White Mountains on the California-Nevada border, and mountain ranges in western Utah. The 38,000-acre **Alta Toquima Wilderness❖** takes its name from the archaeological remains of the highest known Indian village in North America, located on Mount Jefferson.

The last of the four central ranges, the **Monitor Mountains** form a rugged north-south range extending from Route 50 115 miles south to Route 6. In the 98,000-acre **Table Mountain Wilderness❖** are several creeks interspersed with stands of quaking aspen and lush wildflower-filled meadows. Successfully introduced on Table Mountain in 1979, elk have reached a population of approximately 300, and the area supports significant numbers of mule deer, mountain lions, bobcats, coyotes, chukars, blue grouse, and sage grouse. On Table Mountain is a serpentine wall dating back to 50 B.C. that Native Americans used to lure and entrap sage grouse.

Back on Route 50 and 20 miles east of Austin is a small Bureau of Land Management area set aside to protect the **Hickison Petroglyphs❖,** a grouping of Native American rock art set among red volcanic tuff (a short trail leads through sagebrush scrub to the paintings).

THE RUBY MOUNTAINS

Continuing east about 98 miles over basin and range, basin and range, turn off Route 50 onto Route 767 at Moorman Ranch and head north through long, lonesome Long Valley. Just south of Shantytown interpretative signs show where the road crosses the old Overland Stage and Pony Express Route, which was used from 1862 to 1869. After a few miles, the **Ruby Lake National Wildlife Refuge❖** hoves into view. The 37,632-acre refuge encompasses a marsh with dense bulrushes and open water, islands bordered by wet meadows, and grass-sagebrush–covered uplands within the Ruby Valley, a closed drainage basin. In 1827 explorer Jedediah Smith was one of the first nonnatives to see this geographic anomaly—a major wetland surrounded by the

ABOVE: *A sudden storm blankets the arid high country of the Ruby Mountains in a thick cloak of clouds. In the distance, the tops of autumn-tinged aspens seem to stretch skyward for a much-needed drink.*

arid lands of high desert. Eighteen years later John Frémont named the valley after the rubylike garnets he found while charting a new route over the Ruby Mountains, which border the marsh to the west.

During the Pleistocene epoch, the marsh at the Ruby Lake refuge was part of a much larger body of water known as Franklin Lake, which covered about 470 square miles and was more than 200 feet deep. As climatic conditions became warmer and drier, the lake level began to drop. In 1938 the U.S. Fish and Wildlife Service recognized the importance of Ruby Lake as vital habitat for nesting and migratory waterfowl and other birds and wildlife. A collection ditch and a system of dikes were con-

249

structed along the west-central portion of the marsh to collect waters from more than 160 springs on the refuge. The refuge staff tries to mimic the ecological processes of naturally occurring wetlands and uplands.

Visitors can follow a series of dike roads in and around the marsh, and boaters can explore the open water and channels in the bulrushes. Some 200 species of birds have been counted here, including pied-billed grebes, great egrets, sandhill cranes, white-faced ibis, ferruginous hawks, and western kingbirds. Once-endangered trumpeter swans were transplanted here from the Red Rock Lakes National Wildlife Refuge in Montana: Several pairs nest each summer, and 15 or more birds winter here. Also an important breeding ground for two species of ducks, the refuge has produced 3,500 canvasback and 2,500 red-head ducks in good years. Numerous songbird species populate the riparian corridors lining the collection ditch, creek, and spring channels, and yellow-headed blackbirds and barn swallows fill the upland areas.

Eight species of fish swim in the refuge's waters. The relict dace, the only one native to the marsh, is present in just a few other basins in the northeastern corner of the state. Another species, the Lahontan speckled dace, was stocked in the lake in the 1950s. Among other fish plantings are largemouth black bass and rainbow, eastern brook, brown, and cutthroat trout. The marsh supports a number of mammalian species as well, including muskrats, mule deer, and bobcats.

Just north of Ruby Lake is **Franklin Lake,** a 22,000-acre shallow wetland that is important to waterfowl and shorebirds during spring and fall migration. Surrounded by working cattle ranches, it is the largest unprotected wetland ecosystem remaining in the Great Basin. The Nature Conservancy, Nevada Division of Wildlife, American Farmland Trust, and Ducks Unlimited have mounted efforts to preserve and protect it.

Just past the refuge's entrance sign, turn west from Route 767 onto a gravel road and cross over Harrison Pass (7,247 feet) to Route 228. Follow it north and turn east on Route 227 to the Ruby Mountains, arguably the most stunningly scenic of all Nevada's ranges. The entrance to the **Lamoille Canyon Scenic Area❖** passes through the

---

RIGHT: *Snow comes early and stays late on the high peaks towering over Seitz Canyon in the Ruby Mountains. A bristlecone pine and bright yellow wildflower called mule's ears grow among the boulders.*

breathtaking ravine for which it is named.

The ancient walls of Lamoille Canyon began as mud and debris on the floor of an ocean that covered much of western North America 500 million years ago. In time, the sediment was compressed into sedimentary and then metamorphic rocks such as marble and schist. One hundred million years later, molten magma, forced outward from deep inside the earth, melted overlying rock or penetrated into weaker places, eventually hardening as pockets of granite within the older rock. As the earth's crust buckled and wrinkled, the Ruby Mountains were gradually thrust skyward. Since their uplift 15 million years ago, thousands of feet of stone have been eroded by the ravages of wind, rain, and ice, leaving a core of ancient metamorphic rock and its granite intrusions. These form the canyon walls, beribboned by streams of silvery cascading water that turn to sheets of draping ice in winter.

While passing through the canyon, watch for mountain goats and Rocky Mountain bighorn sheep on the high rock ledges. Take the self-guided quarter-mile Changing Canyon Trail, which explains the geologic forces that shaped this unique spot and leads to an active beaver colony. At river's edge American dippers run in and out of the water in pursuit of insects. Across the creek Uinta chipmunks chatter from stands of whitebark pine and aspen. Yellow-bellied marmots scurry along the rocky talus slopes of the north wall, and golden eagles and prairie falcons glide overhead.

At the end of the road is a trailhead for the 40-mile-long **Ruby Crest National Recreation Trail,** an exciting hike traversing the utterly gorgeous and rugged 90,000-acre **Ruby Mountains Wilderness❖.** This magnificent land of jagged spires, glacial tarns, lakes, and cirque basins offers plenty of opportunities for viewing wildlife. One of the more unusual creatures is the Himalayan snow cock, which roosts on talus slopes and forages in tundra meadows.

The Ruby Mountains extend 100 miles and encompass nearly a dozen peaks more than 9,000 feet (the highest is Ruby Dome at 11,387 feet). That height translates into so much precipitation that the Rubies are the wettest range in the state. The upper elevations receive upward of 400 inches of snow a year. The cool, moist climate, in turn, supports plenty of plant communities, some 189 species in the alpine ecosystem alone. There are extensive groves of aspen, as well as a scattering of whitebark and limber pine. The boggy meadows are a paradise for alpine plants, including such classic tundra species as campion and avens—an alpine member of the rose family. Blooming in profusion at lower levels are columbine, corn lilies, coneflowers, bluebells, and forget-me-nots.

NORTH-CENTRAL NEVADA

Backtracking on Route 227, cross Interstate 80 at Elko and take Route 225 north to a signed gravel and dirt road to the Jarbidge Mountains and the 113,000-acre **Jarbidge Wilderness❖.** Similar to the Rubies, the glaciated alpine peaks of the Jarbidge Range—eight exceed 10,000 feet—offer stunning scenery and some of the most remote countryside anywhere. Only a couple of trails penetrate this little-visited range, and the road leading to them is an adventure in itself.

Jarbidge takes its name from a Shoshone Indian legend about Tsaw-Haw-Bitts, an evil ogre that caught people, carried them off to its mountain lair, and devoured them. Eventually the Shoshone lured it into a steep canyon and sealed it in, but the tribe supposedly never returned. European settlers were not put off, however, and in 1909 prospectors struck a vein here, precipitating a gold rush that created a boom town of 1,500. Today, only a handful of hardy residents remain.

The easiest access to the wilderness area is along the Jarbidge River on the Snow Slide Gulch Trail, which passes meadows dotted with colorful wildflowers, rivers thick with rainbow and brook trout, and forests of subalpine fir resembling cathedral spires. Near the tree line, hikers can find a pair of lovely alpine lakes, Jarbidge and Emerald. In autumn changing aspen leaves turn the sides of the Jarbidge Mountains golden, and yellow sunflowers drop their petals in anticipation of the heavy snows of winter, which leave this corner of the state virtually untouched by humans for five months or more.

Due west lies another isolated mountain range and wilderness area in northern Nevada. The **Santa Rosa Mountains❖** and adjoining 31,000-acre **Santa Rosa–Paradise Peak Wilderness❖** are 35 miles north of Winnemucca via Route 95 north and Route 290 northeast (take I-80 from Elko to Winnemucca). Two topographic zones are found here: The southern is marked by steep, rugged granitic formations and high mountain basins, and the northern varies from rather

253

254

flat, broad basins to mesas with basalt outcrops. The equally variable vegetation is typical high-desert Great Basin cover of pinyon-juniper and sagebrush scrub at lower elevations. Deep canyons are lined with riparian vegetation, and quaking aspens, mountain mahogany, and limber pines cling to the higher slopes.

A few hiking trails provide access to the wilderness area, and a 39-mile auto tour penetrates the mountains to the north. Visitors are treated to views of spectacular rock outcroppings, windswept plateaus, and steep mountains while golden eagles and northern goshawks soar on the thermals that billow in front of the outcroppings. Pronghorn and sage grouse frequent the plateaus, but California bighorn sheep stick to the rocky cliffs. Birdlife includes sage grouse, red-shafted flickers, and chukars. The drumming sound in spring comes from ruffed grouse.

Large herds of pronghorn lie 100 miles west near the Oregon border at the **Sheldon National Wildlife Refuge❖,** which can be reached by following Route 95 north and turn-

LEFT: *Meadows spangled with yellow arrowleaf balsam root and purple lupine create a kaleidoscope of colors on the rippled flanks of the Jarbidge Mountains.*

255

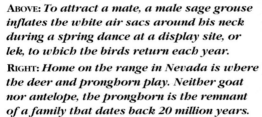

ABOVE: *To attract a mate, a male sage grouse inflates the white air sacs around his neck during a spring dance at a display site, or lek, to which the birds return each year.*

RIGHT: *Home on the range in Nevada is where the deer and pronghorn play. Neither goat nor antelope, the pronghorn is the remnant of a family that dates back 20 million years.*

ing west on Route 140. This sprawling sagebrush-covered expanse, two-thirds the size of Rhode Island, provides habitat for 2,000 of the horned mammals. Although they are often called antelope, pronghorn aren't even related to the antelope family. Pronghorn, endemic to North America, aren't deer, elk, or goats, either. The name comes from the foot-long horns borne by males, which, like antlers, they shed after mating season in fall. Males stand three feet tall and weigh 100 to 150 pounds; females are slightly shorter and about as heavy as a good-sized golden retriever. Reddish brown in color, they sport a black band from eyes to nose, a white throat and stomach, and a white patch on their rump.

Able to run 70 miles per hour in spurts and cruise at 30, pronghorn are speedy enough to outstrip a coyote or bobcat—but not pio-

neers' bullets. Once found by the million throughout the west, they were decimated by hunters and settlers until 1928, when an empty corner of northwestern Nevada was set aside for their protection.

The refuge—named for Charles Sheldon, a hunter and explorer who wrote about the pronghorn in the 1920s—preserves this uniquely North American species and also provides habitat for mule deer, bighorn sheep, coyotes, bobcats, sage grouse, and mountain lions. Scattered springs and lakes attract such migratory waterfowl as Canada geese, mallard, gadwalls, killdeers, and Wilson's phalaropes. Golden eagles, kestrels, and prairie falcons hunt prey ranging from ground squirrels to chukars. Visitors driving through the range should carry plenty of water, make sure their vehicle is in good

working order, and call ahead for weather conditions.

To the south, more pronghorn and other wildlife can be found at the **Soldier Meadows❖,** an area of critical environmental concern. These 5,027 acres are south of the Summit Lake Indian Reservation via a rugged gravel road signed Soldier Meadow that leaves Route 447 ten miles north of Gerlach. In 1843 John Frémont camped here on New Year's Eve, and in 1846 the Applegate brothers pioneered a route nearby which soon became known as the Applegate-Lassen Trail, a historic transportation corridor for pioneers emigrating to Oregon and California. Soldier Meadows is named for the Indian conflicts of the mid-1800s, which in 1866 led to the establishment of cavalry Fort McGarry near Summit Lake to protect Idaho-Nevada stage lines.

A special feature here is the desert aquatic ecosystem. The federally listed threatened desert dace occurs only here, and a rare plant, the basalt cinquefoil (listed as protected) inhabits the hot springs area. Farther north, Summer Camp and Mahogany creeks provide critical spawning habitat for the Lahontan cutthroat, another threatened species.

The Applegate-Lassen Trail leads south, crossing one of the most alien-looking landscapes in the state, the lunarlike silt playa of the **Black Rock Desert❖,** accessed off Route 447 on the outskirts of Gerlach. Follow the turnout onto the desert floor. The desert stretches 60 unbroken miles north to northeast from the town of Gerlach. Flat and white and composed of silt thousands of feet deep in places, it is the ancient bottom of Lake Lahontan.

The dry lake bed is used for numerous recreational events. In 1983 a British racing team set a world record on the playa by driving their four-ton, jet-powered race car more than 633 miles per hour through a measured mile. Visitors like to drive out on the flat playa to test their freedom because the middle of the Black Rock Desert offers the ultimate experience of solitude. On the featureless plain, distance distorts, mirages dance, and the blue sky looks like an infinite dome. On windless days it is so quiet, so still, that the only sounds are the sweeping of a quartz-watch second hand and the beating of the heart.

LEFT: *As clouds scud across the sky, the flat, white salt playa of the Black Rock Desert eventually gives way to the craggy Calico Mountains.*
OVERLEAF: *Tracks that seem to lead nowhere and mountains that hover like a mirage accentuate the lonely emptiness of the Black Rock Desert.*

FURTHER READING ABOUT THE FAR WEST

ALT, DAVID D., AND DONALD HYNDMAN. *Roadside Geology of Northern California*. Missoula, MT: Mountain Press Publishing Company, 1975. This geologic highway guide written for the nonscientist details the ancient marvels still to be seen—even from a car window.

BREWER, WILLIAM HENRY. *Up and Down California in 1860–1864: The Journal of William Henry Brewer*. 1930. Reprint, Berkeley: University of California Press, 1974. Watching grizzlies eat beached whales is just one of the anecdotes in this nonfiction journal by an early California explorer.

BROWER, DAVID. *Not Man Apart*. San Francisco: Sierra Club Books, 1965. A noted California environmentalist combines the poetry of Robinson Jeffers with the photographs of Ansel Adams in this tribute to Big Sur.

CLARK, JEANNE L. *California Wildlife Viewing Guide*. Helena, MT: Falcon Press, 1992. A guide to keep close at hand when exploring parks and nature preserves, with color photos and easy-to-follow directions.

————. *Nevada Wildlife Viewing Guide*. Helena, MT: Falcon Press, 1993. The Silver State's version of the volume described above.

COUGHMAN, MADGE, AND JOANNE S. GINSBURG. *California Coastal Resources Guide*. Berkeley: University of California Press, 1987. Comprehensive resource guide to nearly everything a traveler needs to know about the coastline between Tijuana and the Oregon border.

EVENS, JULES G. *The Natural History of the Point Reyes Peninsula*. Point Reyes, CA: Point Reyes National Seashore Association, 1988. A compendium of essays, natural history, and scientific data with beautiful pen-and-ink drawings by an active field biologist who knows his subject well.

HOLING, DWIGHT. *California Wild Lands: A Guide to The Nature Conservancy Preserves*. San Francisco: Chronicle Books, 1988. A comprehensive guide to the little known and rarely visited private preserves managed by the conservation organization.

MCPHEE, JOHN. *Basin and Range*. New York: Farrar Straus Giroux, 1980. The author's masterful style makes the geologic forces that shaped the Great Basin come alive.

MUIR, JOHN. *My First Summer in the Sierras*. 1911. Reprint, San Francisco: Sierra Club Books, 1990. Muir's sense of wonder and awe is as undying as his spirit in this personal journal.

————. *The Yosemite*. 1912. Reprint, San Francisco: Sierra Club Books. 1988. Muir's eloquent words convinced the public to protect what has become one of the most famous of all national parks.

REISNER, MARC. *Cadillac Desert: The American West and Its Disappearing Water*. New York: Viking, 1986. The story of the relentless quest to control and allocate nature's most precious resource is told with dramatic flair.

STEGNER, WALLACE. *Where the Bluebird Sings to the Lemonade Springs.* New York: Random House, 1992. This master of western literature has authored many books, but this personal look back on living and writing in the West is both evocative and provocative.

STEINHART, PETER. *California's Wild Heritage.* San Francisco: Sierra Club Books, 1990. Color photographs and clearly written descriptions listing the state's threatened and endangered species unfold the hidden message of the consequences of human development.

TRIMBLE, STEPHEN. *The Sagebrush Ocean.* Reno: University of Nevada Press, 1989. The natural histories and mysteries of the Great Basin are revealed in this beautifully written and illustrated oversize book.

ABOVE: *In 1867 Timothy O'Sullivan, who accompanied the Clarence King expedition to survey the 40th parallel, photographed his companions and the sailboat they used to explore Nevada's Truckee River.*

GLOSSARY

anadromous describing those fish that ascend rivers from the sea in order to breed and can live in both salt and fresh water; includes salmon, trout, and shad

badland barren, arid area in which soft rock strata are eroded into varied, fantastic forms

basin depression in the earth's surface; may be created by river drainage, tectonic activity, glacial action, or other natural processes

basin and range description of the topography of the Great Basin region of the West, where depressions in the earth's surface alternate with chains of mountains in a pattern like the folds of an accordion.

butte tall, steep-sided tower of rock formed from an eroded plateau; buttes delay inevitable erosional changes because of their hard uppermost layer of rock

chaparral dense thicket of shrubs or dwarf trees; an ecological community consisting of shrubby plants especially adapted to dry summers and moist winters

cinder cone cone-shaped hill formed from charred lava that builds up around the vent of a volcano

cirque large, bowl-shaped depression in a mountain hollowed out by glacial movement

endemic having originated in and being restricted to one particular environment

escarpment cliff or steep rock face, formed by faulting or fracturing of the earth's crust, that separates two comparatively level land surfaces

estuary region of interaction between ocean water and the end of a river, where tidal action and river flow mix fresh and salt water

fault break in the earth's outermost layer, or crust, along which rock may move against rock, or plate against plate

ferruginous of, or containing, iron; resembling iron rust in color

fumarole hole in a volcanic area from which hot gases and vapors rise

geomorphic relating to the surface features of the earth

grotto artificial structure made to resemble a natural cave

mesa isolated, relatively flat-topped natural elevation more extensive than a butte and less extensive than a plateau

metamorphic referring to rocks that have been changed into their present state after being subjected to heat, pressure, or chemical alteration

midden refuse heap; prehistoric shell middens are often studied by archaeologists to learn about the culture that left them

montane relating to the biogeographic zone of relatively moist, cool upland slopes below timberline; dominated by evergreen trees

pahoehoe satiny, unbroken lava

petroglyph carving on a rock, especially one made by prehistoric people

plate tectonics referring to the changes in the earth's crust, the forces involved, and the resulting formations

pluton formation of lava that cooled before reaching the earth's surface

range chain of mountains

riparian relating to the bank of a natural watercourse, lake, or tidewater

sedimentary referring to rocks formed from deposits of such debris as gravel, sand, mud, silt, or peat

slough swampy, backwater area; inlet on a river; or creek in a marsh or tidal flat

speciation process by which biological populations develop into new species; typically occurs when a small portion of the main population becomes separated by a geographic barrier

subduction tectonic process in which one continental plate is thrust beneath another; generally results in a deep-ocean trench and volcanic arc

talus rock debris that accumulates at the base of a cliff

tarn small, steep-banked mountain lake or pond

timberline boundary that marks the uppermost limit of forest growth on a mountain or at high latitudes; also called the tree line

tufa porous, sedimentary rock formed from calcium carbonate deposited around a spring or along lake shores

wetland area of land covered or saturated with groundwater; includes swamps, marshes, and bogs

ABOVE: *The grandeur of the sequoias, among the world's largest trees, has long drawn tourists to the High Sierra. Here, hats and goggles in place, a family drives through a giant specimen in 1907.*

LAND MANAGEMENT RESOURCES

The following public and private organizations are among the important administrators of the preserved and protected areas described in this volume. Brief explanations of the various legal and legislative designations of these areas follow.

MANAGING ORGANIZATIONS

Bureau of Land Management (BLM) Department of the Interior
Administers nearly half of all federal lands, some 272 million acres. Resources are managed for multiple uses: recreation, grazing, logging, mining, fish and wildlife, and watershed and wilderness preservation.

California Department of Fish and Game The Resource Agency
Responsible for the protection and management of fish and wildlife and threatened native plants. Issues state hunting and fishing licenses.

California Department of Parks and Recreation The Resource Agency.
Manages approximately 1.3 million acres of land consisting of state parks, beaches, and historic sites.

National Oceanic and Atmospheric Administration (NOAA) Department of Commerce
Federal program that oversees U.S. Ocean Service, U.S. Weather Service, marine fisheries, satellite service, and atmospheric research programs.

National Park Service (NPS) Department of the Interior
Regulates the use of national parks, monuments, and preserves. Resources are managed to preserve and protect landscape, natural and historic artifacts, and wildlife. Also administers historic and national landmarks, national seashores, wild and scenic rivers, and the national trail system.

The Nature Conservancy (TNC) Private Organization
International nonprofit organization that owns the largest private system of nature sanctuaries in the world, some 1,300 preserves. Aims to preserve significant and diverse plant, animal, and natural communities. Some areas are managed by other conservation groups, some by the Conservancy itself.

Nevada Division of State Parks Department of Conservation and Natural Resources
Manages 24 state parks totalling 148,563 acres.

US Fish and Wildlife Service (USFWS) Department of the Interior
Principal federal agency responsible for protecting the country's fish and wildlife and their habitats. Manages national wildlife refuges, fish hatcheries, and programs for migratory birds and endangered species.

US Forest Service (USFS) Department of Agriculture
Administers and manages more than 190 million acres in the national forests and national grasslands. Determines how best to combine commercial uses such as grazing, mining, and logging with conservation needs.

DESIGNATIONS

National Conservation Area
Special area set aside by Congress to protect specific environments. May be used for recreation or other specific purposes. Managed by the BLM.

National Estuarine Research Reserve
Established to ensure a stable environment for research through long-term protection of fragile estuarine areas. Managed by NOAA.

National Forest
Large acreage managed for the use of forests, watersheds, wildlife, and recreation by the public and private sectors. Managed by the USFS.

National Marine Sanctuary
Coastal waters protected for their natural, cultural, or historical resources. Restricted fishing, boating, and diving allowed. Managed by NOAA.

National Monument
Nationally significant landmark, structure, object, or area of scientific or historic significance. Managed by NPS.

National Natural Landmark
Nationally significant natural area that is a prime example of a biotic community or a particular geologic feature. Managed by the NPS.

National Park
Primitive or wilderness area with scenery and natural wonders so outstanding it has been preserved by the federal government. Managed by NPS.

National Recreation Area
Site established to conserve and develop for recreational purposes an area of scenic, natural, or historic interest. Power boats, dirt and mountain bikes, and ORVs allowed with restrictions. Managed by the NPS.

National Seashore
Area of pristine undeveloped seashore designated to protect its natural value and provide public recreation. Camping and ORVs allowed with restrictions. Managed by the NPS.

National Wildlife Refuge
Public land set aside for wild animals; protects migratory waterfowl, endangered and threatened species, and native plants. Managed by USFWS.

Natural Area
Area preserved in its natural state for its exceptional value in displaying the natural history of the United States. Managed by individual states.

Natural Preserve
Area that protects specific natural resources. Hunting, fishing, and mining may be permitted. Managed by the NPS and local or state authorities.

Research Natural Area
Land set aside as control area for research on native flora and fauna. Generally open to the public. No vehicles allowed. Managed by the BLM.

Reserve
Area of unique natural features and/or rare and endangered plants and animals protected for conservation and recreation. Generally for day-use only. Managed by individual states.

Wilderness Area
Area with particular ecological, geological, or scientific, scenic, or historical value that has been set aside in its natural condition to be preserved as wild land; limited recreational use is permitted. Managed by BLM and NPS.

NATURE TRAVEL

The following is a selection of national and local organizations that sponsor nature-related travel activities or can provide specialized regional travel information.

NATIONAL

National Audubon Society
700 Broadway
New York, NY 10003
(212) 979-3000
Offers a wide range of ecological field studies, tours, and cruises throughout the United States

National Wildlife Federation
1400 16th Street NW
Washington, D.C. 20036
(703) 790-4363
Offers training in environmental education for all ages, wildlife camp and teen adventures, conservation summits involving nature walks, field trips, and classes

The Nature Conservancy
1815 North Lynn Street
Arlington, VA 22209
(703) 841-5300
Offers a variety of excursions based out of regional and state offices. May include hiking, backpacking, canoeing, horseback riding. Contact above number to locate state offices

Sierra Club Outings
730 Polk Street
San Francisco, CA 94109
(415) 923-5630
Offers tours of different lengths for all ages throughout the United States. Outings may include backpacking, hiking, biking, skiing, and water excursions

Smithsonian Study Tours and Seminars
1100 Jefferson Drive SW
MRC 702
Washington, D.C. 20560
(202) 357-4700
Offers extended tours, cruises, research expeditions, and seminars throughout the United States

REGIONAL

California State Division of Tourism
801 K Street, Suite 1600
Sacramento, CA 95814
(916) 322-2881
(800) 862-2543 (for brochure)
Publishes and distributes travel information package; answers specific questions

Environmental Travelling Companions
Fort Mason Center, Bldg. C
San Francisco, CA 94123
(415) 474-7662
Nonprofit organization offering white-water canoeing, sea kayaking, and cross-country skiing. Special programs for the physically challenged

The Nature Conservancy of Nevada
1771 E. Flamingo, Suite 111B
Las Vegas, NV 89119
(702) 737-8744
Northern Nevada office:
443 Marsh Ave., Reno, NV 89509
(702) 322-4990
Nonprofit environmental organization that conducts hikes and walks throughout Nevada birding areas, wetlands, and paleontological areas; activities in the south are mainly in the spring and summer

Nevada Commission on Tourism
Capitol Complex, Carson City, NV 89710
(800) NEVADA-8 (638-2328)
(800) 237-0774
Publishes and distributes travel brochures; answers specific travel questions

Oceanic Society Expeditions
Fort Mason Center, Bldg. E.
San Francisco, CA 94123
(800) 326-7491
Nonprofit environmental, education, and research organization specializing in naturalist-led marine excursions and research programs

HOW TO USE THIS SITE GUIDE

The following site information guide will assist you in planning your tour of the natural areas of California and Nevada. Sites set in **boldface** and followed by the symbol ❖ in the text are here organized alphabetically by state. Each entry is followed by the mailing address (sometimes different from the street address) and phone number of the immediate managing office, plus brief notes and a list of facilities and activities available. (A key appears on each page.)

Information on hours of operation, seasonal closings, and fees is usually not listed, as these vary from season to season and year to year. Please also bear in mind that responsibility for the management of some sites may change. Call well in advance to obtain maps, brochures, and pertinent, up-to-date information that will help you plan your adventures in the Far West.

Each site entry in the guide includes the address and phone number of its immediate managing agency. Many of these sites are under the stewardship of a forest or park ranger or supervised from a small nearby office. Hence, in many cases, those sites will be difficult to contact directly, and it is preferable to call the managing agency.

The following umbrella organizations can provide general information for individual natural sites, as well as the area as a whole:

CALIFORNIA AND NEVADA

National Park Service Pacific West Field Office
600 Harrison St.
San Francisco, CA 94107
(415) 744-3929

U.S. Fish and Wildlife Service Pacific Regional Office
911 NE 11th Ave.
Portland, OR 97232
(503) 231-6121

CALIFORNIA

Bureau of Land Management
2800 Cottage Way
Sacramento, CA 95825
(916) 979-2805

California Department of Fish and Game
1416 Ninth St.
Sacramento, CA 95814
(916) 653-7664

California Department of Parks and Recreation
1416 Ninth St.
PO Box 94296
Sacramento, CA 94296
(916) 653-4272

The Nature Conservancy
201 Mission St., 4th Floor
San Francisco, CA 94105
(415) 777-0487

NEVADA

Bureau of Land Management
PO Box 12000
Reno, NV 89520
(702) 785-6400

Nevada Division of State Parks
123 W. Nye Ln.
Carson City, NV 89710
(702) 687-4384

U.S. Forest Service
Humboldt and Toiyabe National Forests
1200 Franklin Way
Sparks, NV 89431
(702) 331-6444

CALIFORNIA

AMARGOSA CANYON NATURAL AREA
Bureau of Land Management
Barstow Resource Area
150 Coolwater Lane
Barstow, CA 92311
(619) 255-8700; (619) 256-8313
Be prepared for high summer tempera-
tures, uneven terrain   **BW, H, HR**

**AMBOY CRATER NATIONAL
NATURAL LANDMARK**
Bureau of Land Management
Needles Resource Area
PO Box 888
Needles, CA 92363
(619) 326-3896
No facilities at site   **H**

ANCIENT BRISTLECONE PINE FOREST
Inyo National Forest
White Mountain Ranger District
798 N. Main St.
Bishop, CA 93514
(619) 873-2501
Collecting of bristlecones prohibited
**BW, C, GS, H, I, MT,
PA, RA, T, TG, XC**

ANDREW MOLERA STATE PARK
California Dept. of Parks and Recreation
Big Sur Station #1
Big Sur, CA 93920
(408) 667-2315; (408) 624-7195
**BT, BW, C, F, H, HR,
MB, MT, PA, RA, S, T**

AÑO NUEVO STATE RESERVE
California Dept. of Parks and Recreation
New Year's Creek Rd.
Pescadero, CA 94060
(415) 879-2025
BW, GS, I, MT, RA, T, TG

**ANTELOPE VALLEY
CALIFORNIA POPPY RESERVE**
California Dept. of Parks and Recreation
1051 W. Ave. M
Ste. 201
Lancaster, CA 93534
(805) 942-0662
(805) 724-1180
(818) 768-3533 (wildflower information)
BW, GS, H, I, MT, PA, T, TG

ANZA-BORREGO DESERT STATE PARK
California Dept. of Parks and Recreation
PO Box 299
Borrego Springs, CA 92004
(619) 767-5311 (headquarters)
(619) 767-4205 (visitor center)
(619) 767-4684 (wildflower hotline)
**BT, BW, C, GS, H, HR,
I, MB, MT, PA, RA, T, TG**

**AUDUBON CANYON RANCH–BOLINAS
LAGOON PRESERVE**
4900 Rte. 1
Stinson Beach, CA 94970
(415) 868-9244
BW, GS, H, I, MT, PA, T

BIG BASIN REDWOODS STATE PARK
California Dept. of Parks and Recreation
21600 Big Basin Way
Boulder Creek, CA 95006
(408) 338-6132
Tours during summer only
**BT, BW, C, GS, H, I,
MB, MT, PA, RA, T, TG**

**BIG LAKE–AHJUMAWI LAVA
SPRINGS STATE PARK**
California Dept. of Parks and Recreation
PO Box 942896
Sacramento, CA 94296-0001
(916) 335-2777
Accessible by boat only
BW, C, CK, F, H, PA

BIG MORONGO PRESERVE
Bureau of Land Management
PO Box 2000
North Palm Springs, CA 92258-2000
(619) 343-1234   **BW, H, HR, I, MT, PA**

**BUTTERBREDT SPRING
WILDLIFE SANCTUARY**
The Rudnick Trust
Santa Monica Bay Audubon Society
PO Box 35
Pacific Palisades, CA 90272
Major flyway into the southern Sierra
BW, H

**BUTTE SINK NATIONAL
WILDLIFE REFUGE**
U.S. Fish and Wildlife Service
752 County Rd. 99 W.
Willows, CA 95988
Closed to the public

BT	Bike Trails	**CK**	Canoeing, Kayaking	**F**	Fishing	**HR**	Horseback Riding
BW	Bird-watching			**GS**	Gift Shop		
C	Camping	**DS**	Downhill Skiing	**H**	Hiking	**I**	Information Center

CALAVERAS BIG TREES STATE PARK
California Dept. of Parks and Recreation
PO Box 120, Arnold, CA 95223
(209) 795-2334   **BW, C, F, H, I, MT, PA, RA, S, T, TG, XC**

CASPAR HEADLANDS STATE BEACH AND RESERVE
California Dept. of Parks and Recreation
PO Box 440, Mendocino, CA 95460
(707) 937-5804   **BW, F, S**

CASTLE CRAGS STATE PARK
California Dept. of Parks and Recreation
PO Box 80, Castella, CA 96017
(916) 235-2684   **BW, C, F, H, I, MT, PA, S, T**

CHANNEL ISLANDS NATIONAL MARINE SANCTUARY
National Oceanic and Atmospheric Adm.
113 Harbor Way
Santa Barbara, CA 93109
(805) 966-7107
Whale watching winter and spring; camping permit required
     BW, C, CK, F, I, S, T, TG

CHANNEL ISLANDS NATIONAL PARK
National Park Service
1901 Spinnaker Dr.
Ventura, CA 93001
(805) 658-5700; (805) 658-5730
     BW, C, CK, GS, H, I, MT, PA, RA, S, T, TG

COACHELLA VALLEY PRESERVE
The Nature Conservancy
PO Box 188, Thousand Palms, CA 92276
(619) 343-1234
     BW, H, HR, I, MT, PA, RA, T, TG

COLUSA NATIONAL WILDLIFE REFUGE
U.S. Fish and Wildlife Service
752 County Rd. 99 W., Willows, CA 95988
(916) 934-2801 (916) 934-7774
Auto tour road; information kiosks
     BW, MT

DEATH VALLEY NATIONAL PARK
National Park Service
Death Valley, CA 92328
(619) 786-2331
Mountain bikes allowed on roads only
     BT, BW, C, GS, H, HR, I, L, MT, PA, RA, RC, S, T, TG

DELEVAN NATIONAL WILDLIFE REFUGE
U.S. Fish and Wildlife Service
752 County Rd. Rte. 99 W.
Willows, CA 95988
(916) 934-2801; (916) 934-7774
Limited bird-watching from perimeter county roads
     BW

DEL NORTE COAST REDWOODS STATE PARK
California Dept. of Parks and Recreation
1375 Elk Valley Rd.
Crescent City, CA 95531
(707) 464-9533
     BW, C, H, MB, MT, PA, RA, T

DESERT TORTOISE RESEARCH NATURAL AREA
Bureau of Land Management
300 S. Richmond
Ridgecrest, CA 93555
(619) 384-5400
No motorized vehicles; no dogs
     H, I, MT, T, TG

DESOLATION WILDERNESS
Eldorado National Forest
3070 Camino Heights Dr.
Camino, CA 95709
(916) 644-6048
Wilderness permits required   **F, H, MT**

DEVILS POSTPILE NATIONAL MONUMENT
November through May:
National Park Service
785 N. Main St., Ste. E
Bishop CA 93514
(619) 872-4881
June through October:
PO Box 501, Mammoth Lakes, CA 93546
(619) 934-2289
Includes John Muir, Pacific Crest, Rainbow Falls, and King Creek trails; wilderness permits required for overnight camping   **BW, C, F, H, I, MT, PA, RA, T, TG**

ELKHORN SLOUGH NATIONAL ESTUARINE RESEARCH RESERVE
California Dept. of Fish and Game
1700 Elkhorn Rd.
Watsonville, CA 95076
(408) 728-2822
Closed Monday and Tuesday
     BW, GS, H, I, MT, PA, T, TG

L	Lodging	**PA**	Picnic Areas	**RC**	Rock Climbing	**TG**	Tours, Guides
MB	Mountain Biking	**RA**	Ranger-led Activities	**S**	Swimming	**XC**	Cross-country Skiing
MT	Marked Trails			**T**	Toilets		

EMERALD BAY/D. L. BLISS STATE PARKS
California Dept. of Parks and Recreation
PO Box 266, Tahoma, CA 96142
(916) 525-7277
BW, C, F, H, I, MT, PA, RA, S, T

FISH SLOUGH
Bureau of Land Management
785 North Main St., Ste. E
Bishop, CA 93514
(619) 872-4881   **BW, H, MB**

GARRAPATA STATE PARK
California Dept. of Parks and Recreation
c/o Point Lobos State Reserve
Rte. 1, Box 62
Carmel, CA 93923
(408) 624-4909
Diving; collecting of abalone prohibited;
whale watching in season
BW, F, H, MT, PA, T

GOLDEN GATE NATIONAL RECREATION AREA
National Park Service
Superintendent's Office
Fort Mason, Bldg. 201
San Francisco, CA 94123
(415) 556-0560
Wind surfing; water very cold; dogs
must be on leashes
**BT, BW, C, CK, F, GS, H, HR,
I, MB, MT, PA, RA, S, T, TG**

GRAY DAVIS DYE CREEK PRESERVE
The Nature Conservancy
201 Mission St., 4th Floor
San Francisco, CA 94105
(415) 777-0487
Arrangements must be made with office
before visiting; active cattle ranch operation; visitor season late fall to late spring
BW, T, TG

GRIMSHAW LAKE NATURAL AREA
Bureau of Land Management
Barstow Resource Area
150 Coolwater Lane
Barstow, CA 92311
(619) 255-8760   **BW, H**

GRIZZLY ISLAND STATE WILDLIFE AREA
California Dept. of Fish and Game
2548 Grizzly Island Rd.
Suisun, CA 94585
(707) 425-3828   **BW, F**

GROVER HOT SPRINGS STATE PARK
California Dept. of Parks and Recreation
PO Box 188, Markleeville, CA 96120
(916) 694-2248
Hours of hot springs vary seasonally;
call for hours; fee to use pool
BT, BW, C, F, H, MT, PA, RA, S, T, XC

GUADALUPE–NIPOMO DUNES PRESERVE
The Nature Conservancy
PO Box 15810, San Luis Obispo, CA 93405
(805) 545-9925
Open sunrise to sunset year-round
BW, H, T, TG

HUMBOLDT BAY NATIONAL WILDLIFE REFUGE
U.S. Fish and Wildlife Service
1020 Ranch Rd.
Loleta, CA 95551
(707) 733-5406   **BW, CK, F, H**

HUMBOLDT REDWOODS STATE PARK
California Dept. of Parks and Recreation
PO Box 100, Weott, CA 95571
(707) 946-2409   **BT, BW, C, CK, F, H,
HR, I, MB, MT, PA, RA, S, TG**

JEDEDIAH SMITH REDWOODS STATE PARK
California Dept. of Parks and Recreation
1375 Elk Valley Rd.
Crescent City, CA 95531
(707) 464-9533
BW, C, CK, F, H, I, MB, MT, PA, RA, S, T

JENKINSON LAKE/SLY PARK RECREATION AREA
Eldorado Irrigation District
PO Box 577, Pollack Pines, CA 95726
(916) 644-2545; (916) 644-2792
Tours by prearrangement; entrance fee
**BT, BW, C, CK, F, GS,
H, I, MT, PA, RA, S, T, TG**

JOSHUA TREE NATIONAL PARK
National Park Service
74485 National Park Dr.
Twenty-nine Palms, CA 92277
(619) 367-7511
BW, C, GS, H, I, MT, PA, RA, RC, T, TG

JUG HANDLE STATE RESERVE
California Dept. of Parks and Recreation
PO Box 440, Mendocino, CA 95460
(707) 937-5804
BW, F, H, MT, PA, S

BT Bike Trails	**CK** Canoeing, Kayaking	**F** Fishing	**HR** Horseback Riding	
BW Bird-watching		**GS** Gift Shop		
C Camping	**DS** Downhill Skiing	**H** Hiking	**I** Information Center	

JULIA PFEIFFER BURNS STATE PARK
California Dept. of Parks and Recreation
Big Sur Station #1
Big Sur, CA 93920
(408) 667-2315
Information center at Big Sur Station
BW, C, H, I, L, MT, PA, RA, T

KERN RIVER PRESERVE
The Nature Conservancy
PO Box 1662
Weldon, CA 93283
(619) 378-2531
Call office before visiting; no dogs
BW, I, MT, PA, T

**KINGS CANYON
NATIONAL PARK**
National Park Service
Three Rivers, CA 93271
(209) 565-3134
(209) 565-3351 (recorded weather and
road information)
Seasonal closures; parking precautions,
marmots can damage cars
**BW, C, F, GS, H, HR, I,
L, MT, PA, RA, RC, T, XC**

**KING RANGE NATIONAL
CONSERVATION AREA**
Bureau of Land Management
1695 Heindon Rd.
Arcata, CA 95521
(707) 825-2300; (707) 986-7731
Information center at Shelter Cove; sea-
sonal hours vary
BW, C, F, H, HR, I, MB, MT, PA, T

LAKE TAHOE
U.S. Forest Service
Lake Tahoe Basin Management Unit
870 Emerald Bay Rd.
S. Lake Tahoe, CA 96150
(916) 573-2600
Wilderness permits required
**BT, BW, C, CK, DS, F, H,
HR, I, MB, MT, PA, T, TG, XC**

**LANDELS-HILL BIG
CREEK RESERVE**
University of California
Natural Reserve System
Big Sur, CA 93920
(408) 667-2543
Not open to general public; educational
group tours by prearrangement

LASSEN VOLCANIC NATIONAL PARK
National Park Service
PO Box 100, Mineral, CA 96063-0100
(916) 595-4444
Permits required for overnight travel in
backcountry; no fires in backcountry; no
pets outside developed area
**BW, C, CK, F, GS, H, HR,
I, L, MT, PA, RA, S, T, XC**

LAVA BEDS NATIONAL MONUMENT
National Park Service
PO Box 867, Tulelake, CA 96134
(916) 667-2282
Caving
**BW, C, GS, H, HR, I
MT, PA, RA, T, TG**

**LOS PEÑASQUITOS LAGOON–TORREY
PINES STATE RESERVE**
California Dept. of Parks and Recreation
9609 Waples St., Ste. 200
San Diego, CA 92121
(619) 755-2063
Entrance fee; no dogs; no collecting;
picnic area at beach
**BW, CK, F, GS, H, I, MT,
PA, RA, S, T, TG**

**LOWER KLAMATH NATIONAL
WILDLIFE REFUGE**
U.S. Fish and Wildlife Service
Rte. 1, Box 74, Tulelake, CA 96134
(916) 667-2231
BW, T, TG

MACKERRICHER STATE PARK
California Dept. of Parks and Recreation
PO Box 440
Mendocino, CA 95460
(707) 937-5804
**BT, BW, C, F, H, HR, I, MB,
MT, PA, RA, S, T, TG**

MANILA BEACH AND DUNES
Manila Community Services District
1801 Park St., Arcata, CA 95521
(707) 445-3309
Dune climbing
**BW, CK, F, H, HR, I,
MT, PA, S, T, TG**

**MCARTHUR-BURNEY FALLS MEMORIAL
STATE PARK**
California Dept. of Parks and Recreation
PO Box 942896
Sacramento, CA 94296-0001
(916) 335-2777
BW, C, F, H, I, MT, PA, RA, S, T

L Lodging	**PA** Picnic Areas	**RC** Rock Climbing	**TG** Tours, Guides	
MB Mountain Biking	**RA** Ranger-led Activities	**S** Swimming	**XC** Cross-country Skiing	**273**
MT Marked Trails		**T** Toilets		

THE MECCA HILLS
Bureau of Land Management
Palm Springs–South Coast Resource Area
PO Box 2000
North Palm Springs, CA 92258
(619) 251-4800
Includes Painted Canyon; primitive
camping in wilderness   **BW, C, H, MT**

MENDOCINO HEADLANDS STATE PARK
California Dept. of Parks and Recreation
PO Box 440
Mendocino, CA 95460
(707) 937-5804
BW, F, GS, H, I, PA, T, TG

MOJAVE NATIONAL PRESERVE
National Park Service
150 Coolwater Lane
Barstow, CA 92311
(619) 928-2572 (Hole in the Wall)
(619) 255-8760 (California Desert
Information Center)
Includes Kelso Dunes
BW, C, H, HR, I, MT, PA, RA, T, TG

MONO LAKE
Inyo National Forest
Lee Vining Ranger District
PO Box 429
Lee Vining, CA 93541
(619) 647-3000
Includes Mono Basin Scenic Area Visitor
Center; wilderness permits required;
check in before boating; fishing, swim-
ming, and skiing are at June Lake;
mountain bikes on roads only
**BT, BW, C, CK, DS, F, GS, H, HR,
I, MB, MT, PA, RA, RC, S, T, TG, XC**

MONO LAKE TUFA STATE RESERVE
California Dept. of Parks and Recreation
PO Box 99
Lee Vining, CA 93541
(619) 647-6331   **BW, CK, H, I, MT,
PA, RA, S, T, TG, XC**

MUIR WOODS NATIONAL MONUMENT
National Park Service
Golden Gate National
Recreation Area
Mill Valley, CA 94941
(415) 388-2595 (recording)
(415) 388-2596
Self-guided tours
BW, GS, H, I, MT, RA, T

PFEIFFER BIG SUR STATE PARK
California Dept. of Parks and Recreation
Big Sur Station #1
Big Sur, CA 93920
(408) 667-2315   **BW, C, GS, H, I, L,
MT, PA, RA, S, T**

POINT LOBOS STATE RESERVE
California Dept. of Parks and Recreation
Rte. 1, Box 62
Carmel, CA 93923
(408) 624-4909
Day use only; no collecting; no dogs
BW, H, I, MT, PA, T, TG

POINT REYES NATIONAL SEASHORE
National Park Service
Point Reyes Station, CA 94956
(415) 663-1092
Backpack camping
**BT, BW, C, CK, F, GS, H,
HR, I, MT, PA, RA, S, T**

PRAIRIE CREEK REDWOODS STATE PARK
California Dept. of Parks and Recreation
15336 Hwy. 101
Trinidad, CA 95570
(707) 488-2171   **BT, BW, C, H, I, MB,
MT, PA, RA, T**

PROVIDENCE MOUNTAINS STATE
RECREATION AREA
California Dept. of Parks and Recreation
Angeles District, Mojave Desert Sector
1051 W. Ave. M, Ste. 201
Lancaster, CA 93534
(805) 942-0662
(619) 255-8760 (Desert Information Center)
Includes Mitchell Caverns
BW, C, GS, H, I, MT, PA, RA, T, TG

RED ROCK CANYON STATE PARK
California Dept. of Parks
and Recreation
PO Box 26
Cantil, CA 93519
(805) 942-0662
BW, C, GS, H, I, PA, RA, T

REDWOOD NATIONAL PARK
National Park Service
1111 Second St.
Crescent City, CA 95531
(707) 464-6101
**BT, BW, C, CK, F, H, HR, I,
MB, MT, PA, RA, S, T, TG**

BT	Bike Trails	**CK**	Canoeing, Kayaking	**F**	Fishing	**HR**	Horseback Riding
BW	Bird-watching			**GS**	Gift Shop		
C	Camping	**DS**	Downhill Skiing	**H**	Hiking	**I**	Information Center

RUSSIAN GULCH STATE PARK
California Dept. of Parks and Recreation
PO Box 440, Mendocino, CA 95460
(707) 937-5804
BT, BW, C, F, H, MB, MT, PA, RA, S, T

SACRAMENTO NATIONAL WILDLIFE REFUGE COMPLEX
U.S. Fish and Wildlife Service
752 County Rd. Rte. 99 W.
Willows, CA 95988
(916) 934-2801; (916) 934-7774
Wildlife viewing platform; auto tour road; need two weeks' advance notice to arrange group programs
BW, I, MT, RA, T, TG

SACRAMENTO RIVER REFUGE
U.S. Fish and Wildlife Service
752 County Rd. Rte. 99 W.
Willows, CA 95988
(916) 934-2801; (916) 934-7774
BW, MT

SADDLEBACK BUTTE STATE PARK
California Dept. of Parks and Recreation
1051 W. Ave. M, Ste. 201
Lancaster, CA 93534
(805) 942-0662
BW, C, H, MT, PA, RA, T

SALTON SEA NATIONAL WILDLIFE REFUGE
U.S. Fish and Wildlife Service
PO Box 120
Calipatria, CA 92233
(619) 348-5278; (619) 348-5310
Tours by prearrangement
BW, H, I, MT, PA, T

SALTON SEA RECREATION AREA
California Dept. of Parks and Recreation
100-225 State Park Rd.
North Shore, CA 92254
(619) 393-3052
BW, C, F, GS, I, PA, RA, S, T

SALT POINT STATE PARK
California Dept. of Parks and Recreation
25050 Coast Hwy. One
Jenner, CA 95450
(707) 847-3221
Biking May through October on fire roads only; no form of marine life may be taken or disturbed within Gerstle Cove Reserve
BT, BW, C, F, H, MB, MT, PA, T

SANTA MONICA MOUNTAINS NATIONAL RECREATION AREA
National Park Service
30401 Agoura Rd., Ste. 100
Agoura Hills, CA 91301
(818) 597-9192
Pets must be on leashes
BT, BW, C, GS, H, HR, I, MB, MT, PA, RA, T

SEQUOIA NATIONAL PARK
National Park Service
Three Rivers, CA 93271
(209) 565-3134
(209) 565-3351 (recorded weather and road information updated 9 A.M. daily)
Seasonal closures
BW, C, F, GS, H, HR, I, L, MT, PA, RA, RC, T, XC

SINKYONE WILDERNESS STATE PARK
California Dept. of Parks and Recreation
PO Box 245, Whitethorn, CA 95589
(707) 986-7711
Limited vehicle access; 4WD may be required in wet weather
BW, C, F, H, I, MT, T

SUTTER NATIONAL WILDLIFE REFUGE
U.S. Fish and Wildlife Service
752 County Rd. Rte. 99 W.
Willows, CA 95988
(916) 934-2801; (916) 934-7774
Limited bird-watching from county road that bisects refuge
BW

TIJUANA RIVER NATIONAL ESTUARINE RESEARCH RESERVE
U.S. Fish and Wildlife Service
Southern California Coastal Complex
2736 Loker Ave. W., Ste. A
Carlsbad, CA 92008
(619) 575-2704; (619) 930-0168
Includes Tijuana Slough National Wildlife Refuge; many areas are sensitive and closed to public entry, check with office
BT, BW, GS, H, HR, I, MT, T

TRONA PINNACLES NATIONAL NATURAL LANDMARK
Bureau of Land Management
Ridgecrest Resource Area
300 S. Richmond, Ridgecrest, CA 93555
(619) 384-5400
Primitive camping
C, H, HR, MB, FC

L	Lodging	PA	Picnic Areas	RC	Rock Climbing	TG Tours, Guides
MB	Mountain Biking	RA	Ranger-led Activities	S	Swimming	XC Cross-country Skiing
MT	Marked Trails			T	Toilets	

TULE LAKE NATIONAL WILDLIFE REFUGE
U.S. Fish and Wildlife Service
Rte. 1, Box 74, Tulelake, CA 96134
(916) 667-2231
BW, CK, GS, I, MT, PA, T, TG

**UPPER NEWPORT BAY ECOLOGICAL
RESERVE**
California Dept. of Fish and Game
600 Shellmaker Rd.
Newport Beach, CA 92660
(714) 640-6746
Fishing restricted to certain areas; tours
by prearrangement
BW, CK, F, H, HR, I, MB, MT, RA, T, TG

VENTANA WILDERNESS AREA
Los Padres National Forest
Monterey Ranger District
406 S. Mildred, King City, CA 93930
(408) 385-5434
Camping permit required
BW, C, F, H, HR, I, T

VINA PLAINS PRESERVE
The Nature Conservancy
201 Mission St., 4th Floor
San Francisco, CA 94105
(415) 777-0487
Arrangements must be made with office
before visiting; best time for wildflowers
February through early May; no pets; no
smoking **BW, TG**

WESTPORT–UNION LANDING STATE BEACH
California Dept. of Parks and Recreation
PO Box 440; Mendocino, CA 95460
(707) 937-5804 **C, F, PA, T**

YOSEMITE NATIONAL PARK
National Park Service
PO Box 577
Yosemite, CA 95389
(209) 372-0200
(209) 372-0265 (recording)
Wilderness permits required for
overnight camping
**BT, BW, C, DS, F, GS, H, HR, I, L,
MT, PA, RA, RC, S, T, TG, XC**

NEVADA

ALTA TOQUIMA WILDERNESS
Toiyabe National Forest
Tonopah Ranger District
PO Box 3940, Tonopah, NV 89049
(702) 482-6286 **BW, C, F, H, HR**

ANAHO NATIONAL WILDLIFE REFUGE
U.S. Fish and Wildlife Service
PO Box 1236; Fallon, NV 89406
(702) 423-5128
Closed to the public

ARC DOME WILDERNESS
Toiyabe National Forest
Tonopah Ranger District
PO Box 3940, Tonopah, NV 89049
(702) 482-6286 **BW, C, F, H, HR**

**ASH MEADOWS
NATIONAL WILDLIFE REFUGE**
U.S. Fish and Wildlife Service
PO Box 2660, Pahrump, NV 89041
(702) 372-5435
Desert heat in summer; bring water;
tours by prearrangement
BW, H, I, T, TG

BERLIN-ICHTHYOSAUR STATE PARK
Nevada Div. of State Parks
HC 61, Box 61200
Austin, NV 89310-9301
(702) 964-2440
Removal of artifacts prohibited; pets
must be on leashes
BW, C, I, MT, PA, RA, T, TG

BLACK ROCK DESERT
Bureau of Land Management
Sonoma-Gerlach Resource Area
705 E. 4th St., Winnemucca, NV 89445
(702) 623-1500 **C,H, HR, I, MB**

CATHEDRAL GORGE STATE PARK
Nevada Div. of State Parks
PO Box 176, Panaca, NV 89042
(702) 728-4467 **BW, C, H, I, MT, PA, T**

CAVE LAKE STATE PARK
Nevada Div. of State Parks
PO Box 761, Ely, NV 89301
(702) 728-4467
Ice fishing
BW, C, CK, F, H, PA, T, XC

DESERT NATIONAL WILDLIFE RANGE
U.S. Fish and Wildlife Service
1500 N. Decatur Blvd.
Las Vegas, NV 89108
(702) 646-3401
High clearance or 4WD vehicles recom-
mended; bring water
BW, C, H, HR, I

BT	Bike Trails	**CK**	Canoeing, Kayaking	**F**	Fishing	**HR**	Horseback Riding
BW	Bird-watching			**GS**	Gift Shop		
C	Camping	**DS**	Downhill Skiing	**H**	Hiking	**I**	Information Center

GALENA CREEK PARK
Washoe County Parks and
Recreation Dept.
PO Box 11130, Reno, NV 89520
(702) 849-2511
Hours vary seasonally
BW, F, H, HR, MT, PA, RA, T, XC

GREAT BASIN NATIONAL PARK
National Park Service
Baker, NV 89311-9701
(702) 234-7331
Includes Lehman Caves, Lexington Arch,
Bristlecone Pine Forest, and three camp-
grounds; high-elevation precautions; fee
to enter caves
**BW, C, F, GS, H, HR, I, MT,
PA, RA, T, TG, XC**

HICKISON PETROGLYPHS
Bureau of Land Management
PO Box 911
Tonopah, NV 89049
(702) 482-7800
Primitive camping and hiking; bring
water **C, H, HR, MB, MT, T**

JARBIDGE WILDERNESS
Humboldt National Forest
2035 Last Chance Rd.
Elko, NV 89801
(702) 738-5171
Some trailheads accessible only with
4WD **BW, C, F, H, HR, MT, PA**

LAKE MEAD NATIONAL RECREATION AREA
National Park Service
601 Nevada Hwy.
Boulder City, NV 89005
(702) 293-8907; (702) 293-8990
Boat rentals; waterskiing; dogs allowed
on leashes **BW, C, CK, F, GS, H, I,
L, PA, RA, S, T, TG**

LAKE TAHOE–NEVADA STATE PARK
Nevada Div. of State Parks
PO Box 8867
Incline Village, NV 89452-8867
(702) 831-0494
Includes Marlette Lake, Tunnel Creek,
Spooner Lake, Hobart Creek Reservoir,
Twin Lakes, Sand Harbor, and Cave
Rock; no fishing in Marlette Lake; primi-
tive camping; seasonal fees
**BT, BW, F, H, HR,
I, MT, PA, S, T**

LAMOILLE CANYON SCENIC AREA
Humboldt National Forest
PO Box 246, Wells, NV 89835
(702) 752-3357
(800) 764-3359 (Nevada only)
Road not maintained in winter months
BW, C, F, H, HR, MB, MT, PA, T, XC

**MOAPA VALLEY
NATIONAL WILDLIFE REFUGE**
U.S. Fish and Wildlife Service
1500 N. Decatur Blvd., Las Vegas, NV 89108
(702) 646-3401 **BW, PA, T**

MOUNT ROSE WILDERNESS
Toiyabe National Forest
Carson Ranger District
1200 Franklin Way, Sparks, NV 89431
(702) 355-5300; (702) 882-2766
BW, C, H, HR, MT, XC

**PAHRANAGAT
NATIONAL WILDLIFE REFUGE**
U.S. Fish and Wildlife Service
PO Box 510, Alamo, NV 89001
(702) 725-3417 **BW, C, F, H, PA, T**

PYRAMID LAKE
Paiute Tribe
PO Box 256, Nixon, NV 89424
(702) 574-1000
Includes Pyramid Lake Marina, Numana
Hatchery, and Pyramid Lake Fisheries
C, F, GS, I, PA, S, TG

**RED ROCK CANYON NATIONAL
CONSERVATION AREA**
Bureau of Land Management
4765 Vegas Dr.
Las Vegas, NV 89108
(702) 363-1921
**BT, BW, C, GS, H, HR, I,
MT, PA, RA, RC, T**

REDSTONE PICNIC AREA
National Park Service
Lake Mead National Recreation Area
601 Nevada Hwy.
Boulder City, NV 89005
(702) 293-8907 **BW, MT, PA, T**

RUBY LAKE NATIONAL WILDLIFE REFUGE
U.S. Fish and Wildlife Service
HC 60, Box 860
Ruby Valley, NV 89833-9802
(702) 779-2237
Self-guided auto tour **BW, C, CK, F, I, T**

L Lodging	**PA** Picnic Areas	**RC** Rock Climbing	**TG** Tours, Guides
MB Mountain Biking	**RA** Ranger-led Activities	**S** Swimming	**XC** Cross-country Skiing
MT Marked Trails		**T** Toilets	

277

RUBY MOUNTAINS WILDERNESS
U.S. Forest Service
Ruby Mountains Ranger District
PO Box 246
Wells, NV 89835
(702) 752-3357
(800) 764-3359 (Nevada only)
No motorized equipment allowed; facilities at Roads End trailhead
BW, C, F, H, HR, MT, RC

SANTA ROSA MOUNTAINS
Humboldt National Forest
Santa Rosa Ranger District
1200 E. Winnemucca Blvd.
Winnemucca, NV 89445
(702) 623-5025
BW, C, F, GS, H, HR, I, MB, PA, T, XC

SANTA ROSA–PARADISE PEAK WILDERNESS
Humboldt National Forest
Santa Rosa Ranger District
1200 E. Winnemucca Blvd.
Winnemucca, NV 89445
(702) 623-5025
Gravel auto-tour route not open in winter
BW, C, F, H, HR

SHELDON NATIONAL WILDLIFE REFUGE
U.S. Fish and Wildlife Service
PO Box 111
18 South G
Lakeview, OR 97630
(503) 947-3315
Roads through refuge are closed during winter
BW, C, F, H, HR

SOLDIER MEADOWS
Bureau of Land Management
Sonoma-Gerlach Resource Area
705 E. 4th St.
Winnemucca, NV 89445
(702) 623-1500
Fragile area; public access may be limited
H

SPRING MOUNTAIN RANCH
Nevada Div. of State Parks
PO Box 124
Blue Diamond, NV 89004
(702) 875-4141
Day use only
BT, BW, GS, H, HR, I, MB, PA, RA, T, TG

SPRING MOUNTAINS NATIONAL RECREATION AREA
Toiyabe National Forest
2881 S. Valley Blvd., Ste. 16
Las Vegas, NV 89102
(702) 873-8800
(702) 222-1597 (recorded information)
Includes Mount Charleston Wilderness and Charleston Peak
BW, C, DS, H, HR, I, L, MB, MT, PA, RC, T, XC

STILLWATER NATIONAL WILDLIFE REFUGE
U.S. Fish and Wildlife Service
PO Box 1236
Fallon, NV 89407
(702) 423-5128
BW, C, F

TABLE MOUNTAIN WILDERNESS
Toiyabe National Forest
Tonopah Ranger District
PO Box 3940
Tonopah, NV 89049
(702) 482-6286
BW, C, F, H, HR

TOIYABE NATIONAL FOREST
U.S. Forest Service
1200 Franklin Way
Sparks, NV 89431
(702) 331-6444
Includes Mount Rose Wilderness; high-elevation precautions; Sierra passes subject to winter closures
BW, C, DS, H, HR, I, XC

VALLEY OF FIRE STATE PARK
Nevada Div. of State Parks
PO Box 515
Overton, NV 89040
(702) 397-2088
BW, C, GS, H, I, MB, MT, PA, T

WALKER LAKE
Bureau of Land Management
1535 Hot Springs Rd.
Carson City, NV 89706
(702) 885-6000
Includes Sportsmens Beach; no water available
BW, C, CK, F, H, HR, MB, PA, S, T

WASHOE LAKE STATE PARK
Nevada Div. of State Parks
4855 East Lake Blvd.
Carson City, NV 89704
(702) 687-4319
BT, BW, C, CK, F, H,

BT	Bike Trails	**CK**	Canoeing, Kayaking	**F**	Fishing	**HR**	Horseback Riding
BW	Bird-watching	**DS**	Downhill Skiing	**GS**	Gift Shop	**I**	Information Center
C	Camping			**H**	Hiking		

ABOVE: *Seen here in an 1800s lithograph, the giant sequoia was first simply called the Big Tree. British botanists named it* Wellingtonia *for the duke; the botanical name Americans chose,* Sequoiadendron giganteum, *now prevails.*

L	Lodging	**PA**	Picnic Areas	**RC**	Rock Climbing	**TG**	Tours, Guides
MB	Mountain Biking	**RA**	Ranger-led Activities	**S**	Swimming	**XC**	Cross-country Skiing
MT	Marked Trails			**T**	Toilets		

INDEX

PHOTOGRAPH CREDITS

All photography by Diane Cook and Len Jenshel except for the following:

i: Tom and Pat Leeson, Vancouver, WA
iv: Carr Clifton, Taylorsville, CA
viii, right: Erwin and Peggy Bauer, Livingston, MT
ix, right: Zig Leszczynski/Animals Animals, Chatham, NY
xiv–xv: Collection of the Oakland Museum of California, Gift of Miss Marguerite Laird in memory of Mr. and Mrs. P.W. Laird
xvi: Willard Clay, Ottawa, IL
9: Larry Ulrich, Trinidad, CA
12: Thomas D. Mangelsen/Images of Nature, Jackson, WY
13: Jeff Foott, Jackson, WY
15: Larry Ulrich, Trinidad, CA
20–21: David Muench, Santa Barbara, CA
23, 25, bottom: John Cancalosi, Tucson, AZ
27: Erwin and Peggy Bauer, Livingston, MT
28: Jeff Foott, Jackson, WY
29: James Cornett, Palm Springs, CA
34: Zig Leszczynski/Animals Animals, Chatham, NY
37, 40–41: David Muench, Santa Barbara, CA
49: Mark Lewis/West Stock, Seattle, WA
50–51: Zandria Muench Beraldo, Santa Barbara, CA
52: Marc Muench, Santa Barbara, CA
56–57: David Muench, Santa Barbara, CA
59: Larry Ulrich, Trinidad, CA
61: Carr Clifton, Taylorsville, CA
62: Wendy Shattil and Bob Rozinski, Denver, CO
63: Galen Rowell/Mountain Light, Albany, CA
64: Larry Ulrich, Trinidad, CA
66–67: David Muench, Santa Barbara, CA
68: Culver Pictures, Inc., New York, NY
70, 71, top left: John Gerlach, Chatham, MI
71, bottom left: Bates Littlehales, Arlington, VA
71, right: John Gerlach, Chatham, MI
73: Carr Clifton, Taylorsville, CA
74: Tim Thompson, Bainbridge Island, WA
75: John Hendrickson, Clipper Mills, CA
76: John Cancalosi, Tucson, AZ
88: Erwin and Peggy Bauer, Livingston, MT
91: John Hendrickson, Clipper Mills, CA
98: Thomas D. Mangelsen/Images of Nature, Jackson, WY
99, top: Alan and Sandy Carey, Bozeman, MT
99, bottom: John Shaw, Colorado Springs, CO
102, 103: Library of Congress, Washington, D.C.
107: Wendy Shattil and Bob Rozinski, Denver, CO
108: Tom and Pat Leeson, Vancouver, WA
110: Tom Bean, Flagstaff, AZ
112: John Hendrickson, Clipper Mills, CA
113: Erwin and Peggy Bauer, Livingston, MT
114: John Cancalosi, Tucson, AZ
123: Thomas D. Mangelsen/Images of Nature, Jackson, WY
138: Jeff Foott, Jackson, WY

143, top: Tom and Pat Leeson, Vancouver, WA
143, bottom: Arthur Morris/Birds As Art, Deltona, FL
147: Larry Ulrich, Trinidad, CA
148: Tom and Pat Leeson, Vancouver, WA
149: Erwin and Peggy Bauer, Livingston, MT
154: Larry Ulrich, Trinidad, CA
156: Jeffrey Rich, Millville, CA
158: Erwin and Peggy Bauer, Livingston, MT
160, 161: Jeff Foott, Jackson, WY
168: Larry Ulrich, Trinidad, CA
169: Zig Leszczynski/Animals Animals, Chatham, NY
181: Jeff Foott, Jackson, WY
182, 190: George H.H. Huey, Prescott, AZ
192: Howard G. Booth, Boulder, NV
195: Tom Bean, Flagstaff, AZ
200–201: David Muench, Santa Barbara, CA
202: Zig Leszczynski/Animals Animals, Chatham, NY
203, top: John Cancalosi, Tucson, AZ
203, bottom: Zig Leszczynski/Animals Animals, Chatham, NY
208, left: George H.H. Huey, Prescott, AZ
210: Wendy Shattil and Bob Rozinski, Denver, CO
211, top left: John Cancalosi, Tucson, AZ
211, bottom left: Bates Littlehales, Arlington, VA
211, right: Wendy Shattil and Bob Rozinski, Denver, CO
215: John Gerlach, Chatham, MI
221: Tom Bean, Flagstaff, AZ
224: Scott T. Smith, North Logan, UT
232, left: Erwin and Peggy Bauer, Livingston, MT
234: National Archives, Washington, D.C., (#AM.IM.27)
238, left: Tom and Pat Leeson, Vancouver, WA
239, bottom, 241: Tom Bean, Flagstaff, AZ
244, top: Wendy Shattil and Bob Rozinski, Denver, CO
244, bottom: Tim Fitzharris/Masterfile, Toronto, Canada
245: Thomas D. Mangelsen/Images of Nature, Jackson, WY
247: John Cancalosi, Tucson, AZ
251, 254–255: David Muench, Santa Barbara, CA
256, left: Michael H. Francis, Billings, MT
256–257: Bates Littlehales, Arlington, VA
263: Library of Congress, Washington, D.C. (LC-USZ62-22282)
265: Library of Congress, Washington, D.C. (LC-USZ62-58968Q)
279: Library of Congress, Washington, D.C.
Back Cover: Len Jenshel (Elephant Rock); John Cancalosi (prickly pear cactus); Tim Thompson (mountain lion)

ACKNOWLEDGMENTS

The editors gratefully acknowledge the professional assistance of Susan Kirby and Patricia Woodruff. The following consultants also helped in the preparation of this volume: Glenn H. Clemmer, Nevada Department of Conservation and Natural Resources; John E. Grassy; Stephen J. Nicola, Senior Biologist, Lands and Natural Areas PRogram Coordinator, California Department of Fish and Game; and Dallas Rhodes, Professor and Chair of Geology, Whittier College, CA.